Listening Is Learning

Also by Frank Thoms
Exciting Classrooms: Practical Information to Ensure Student Success
Teaching that Matters: Engaging Minds, Improving Schools

Listening Is Learning

Conversations between 20th and 21st Century Teachers

Frank Thoms

ROWMAN & LITTLEFIELD
Lanham • Boulder • New York • London

Published by Rowman & Littlefield
An imprint of The Rowman & Littlefield Publishing Group, Inc.
4501 Forbes Boulevard, Suite 200, Lanham, Maryland 20706
www.rowman.com

6 Tinworth Street, London SE11 5AL, United Kingdom

Copyright © 2019 by Frank Thoms

All rights reserved. No part of this book may be reproduced in any form or by any electronic or mechanical means, including information storage and retrieval systems, without written permission from the publisher, except by a reviewer who may quote passages in a review.

British Library Cataloguing in Publication Information Available

Library of Congress Cataloging-in-Publication Data
Names: Thoms, Frank, 1938- editor.
Title: Listening is learning : conversations between 20th and 21st century teachers / [edited by] Frank Thoms.
Description: Lanham, Maryland : Rowman & Littlefield, [2018] | Includes bibliographical references and index.
Identifiers: LCCN 2018034745 (print) | LCCN 2018047100 (ebook) | ISBN 9781475840155 (electronic) | ISBN 9781475840131 (cloth : alk. paper) | ISBN 9781475840148 (pbk. : alk. paper)
Subjects: LCSH: Effective teaching. | Teachers—Professional relationships. | Mentoring in education.
Classification: LCC LB1025.3 (ebook) | LCC LB1025.3 . L564 2018 (print) | DDC 371.102—dc23
LC record available at https://lccn.loc.gov/2018034745

∞™ The paper used in this publication meets the minimum requirements of American National Standard for Information Sciences—Permanence of Paper for Printed Library Materials, ANSI/NISO Z39.48-1992.

Printed in the United States of America

We came upon a group of men. They wore long rubber boots and stood knee-deep in the water.

"These men," de Kooning said, "they come here and throw in a line to see if they can catch a fish. Most of the time, they never do. I know they don't care, because it's like make-believe. Except, the fisherman has to believe he might catch one. So he has to do his best, otherwise it doesn't count.

"So I come here to look at them not catching fish but believing it's possible, and I feel so good here, because painting is make-believe, too, where I'm also trying to do the impossible."

One of the fisherman turned and waved. De Kooning waved back.

"You see?" he said smiling. "We both know it's impossible. But it doesn't matter, as long as we believe it might be possible one day."

—Willem de Kooning, interview in *The New York Times*, November 20, 1983. Kindness of Sarah Ritter, a former colleague who wrote, "I read this and thought of you . . . and all of us smiled."

Contents

Preface		ix
Acknowledgments		xiii
1	Break the Mold: Michael Harding and Meera Sharma	1
2	Engage Students: Michael Harding and Meera Sharma	9
3	Invoke Primary Sources: Frances Smith and Joyce Bertrand	15
4	Frame the Big Picture: Michael Harding, Frances Smith, Meera Sharma, and Joyce Bertrand	25
5	Teach Students to Think: Terry Rowe and Ivan Deutsch	33
6	Explore the Other Side: Terry Rowe and Ivan Deutsch	41
7	Using Grading to Improve Learning: George Persons and Harold Coughlin	51
8	Co-Teach with a Master Teacher: Del Goodwin and Lewis Denton	59
9	Teach Collaboratively: Paula Ralston, Jennifer Symons, and Jeremy Wilson	65
10	Embrace Controversy: Martin Oldenberg, Ellen Harper, and Isabella Gonzalez	75
11	Teach Reading for Understanding: Carolyn Hench and Lea Archer	87
12	Invest in Social-Emotional Learning: George Persons, Harold Coughlin, and Amanda Booker	95

13 To Google or Not to Google: Don Jorgensen, Amy Watson, Gordon Mason, and Bonnie Canton	103
14 Stay Grounded in Reality: Don Jorgensen, Amy Watson, Gordon Mason, and Bonnie Canton	113
15 Seek the Middle Ground: Martin Oldenberg, Ellen Harper, Isabella Gonzalez, and Thomas Singleton	123
16 And It's the Little Things: Lillian Bailey, Michael Harding, Meera Sharma, John Hutchinson, Ford Daley, and Martha Esersky	131
Coda	137
Appendix	139
Index	145
About the Author	155

Preface

You can't do it alone. Yet it's one of the practices expected of you. School opens. You're in your classroom. Students pour in. You think you'll handle it. You are quaking in your shoes. Today is your wake-up call. You've decided to teach. Now you will—or hope you will.

To do it alone is difficult. Teaching is enormously complex, involving multiple decisions about students, curriculum, colleagues, and yourself. Your school, a private world, separate from society, a fiefdom within its castle walls. Its schedule dictates. The bell rings. Students fill the hallways. The bell rings again. The halls go silent. You teach. The bell again. You anticipate the next group, and the next, and the next. It's lunch, and afterward you spur into action. Then the final bell rings. You collapse in your chair and wonder what's happened—and it's only been one day.

Whatever has been your first day—or will be—you will most likely be alone. You likely practice taught for six weeks, perhaps with guidance, perhaps not. You have your certificate. You've signed a contract. You've been through induction and may have a mentor. You close the door to your classroom. You're on your own.

Listening Is Learning: Conversations between 20th and 21st Century Teachers invites you to step outside what may feel like an imposed cocoon. Seek the knowledge and advice of former teachers, retired educators, and respected veterans. Search for their best ideas, methods, materials, insights. Ask them to share moments of success, epiphanies, methodologies, and certainly their struggles. Let them into your life. You'll become a better teacher.

Don't succumb to meaningless routines. Find procedures that work to facilitate your purposes. Do you remember teachers who structured their classes the same every day? The math teacher who began every lesson having homework put on the board: she would go over it, collect it, introduce the next concept in the textbook, allow time to start homework, and dismiss at the bell. You don't need to be like that. Be yourself. Teach from your heart.

Seek the advice of the greats before you. Everyone knows who they are. Look for them. Contact them. As I've said, you'll become a better teacher. In *Listening Is Learning*, you will observe twentieth-century teachers who offer exciting ways to help you in the twenty-first century. You'll discover better ways to engage your digitally driven, distracted students. You'll meet Michael Harding, retired, who shares stories about his first year in his classroom with new teacher Meera Sharma. He devised simple changes from traditional practice, the most significant: abandoning desks in rows.

You'll meet Frances Smith and young teacher Joyce Bertrand. Mrs. Smith shares her distaste for textbooks and offers multiple ways to engage active learning. Terry Rowe meets with new teacher Ivan Deutsch and shares his Cold War–era teaching of Marxism, communism, and the Soviet Union to eighth graders. Ivan plans to adopt some of Mr. Rowe's methods to engage and immerse his students. And you'll read about Ellen Harper, who learns from Martin Oldenberg about using Edward de Bono's Six Hats in her classroom.

And you'll meet others: retired teachers, veterans, and fellow new teachers. By the time you've finished this book, you will understand that teaching is a collaborative process. You are one in a long line of teachers before you. Pay attention to these conversations. Observe new teachers learning from veterans and veterans learning from new teachers. Great teachers learn from anyone all the time. A caution: Don't make the Internet your sole companion. You'll find lessons that are potshots, shallow, decontextualized, instant-set activities, and space fillers. You might be lucky to find some good ideas, but nothing replaces conversations like the ones you'll read about here.

As a longtime teacher, I've argued that building camaraderie with fellow teachers, especially ones that can mentor, is essential. Being alongside veteran Del Goodwin, first-year teacher Lewis Denton has his eyes and mind open to possibilities. Imagine what you could glean working with such a teacher. Imagine, too, someday, becoming a Mr. Goodwin yourself, lifting a new colleague onto her feet.

Be willing to take responsibility for your profession. As a young teacher, in seeking the advice of educators who came before you, you stand on their shoulders, as I did on the shoulders of those before me. Soon it will be your turn to offer your shoulders to a younger colleague.

Before writing this book I considered answering the question: What will make for a great twenty-first-century teacher? As I started to write, I recollected that I could not possibly have known what I needed to become great in my time. I began teaching in the 1960s, having had a conservative, liberal arts education. It was a fixed worldview leading women to become teachers and nurses, and men professors, lawyers, doctors, and businessmen. I became a teacher; there weren't many men before me.

If you stepped into my well-heeled high school in 1969, nearly a decade after I arrived, you'd think you were in a different school. The dress code disappeared, girls went braless, boys wore bellbottoms, there was more pushback from students, and teachers came into school stoned. The 1960s culture burst upon us, forcing us to rethink our approaches: the Cuban missile crisis, JFK's assassination, civil rights, Martin Luther King Jr. and Robert Kennedy assassinations, Vietnam, feminism, gay rights, Ed Sullivan, the Beatles, Woodstock, and putting a man on the moon. Other changes happened over my fifty years of teaching in public, private, and international schools and serving as an educational consultant—all of which demanded creative pedagogies.

In this book, I offer you effective, engaging practices, many of which I've leveraged from teachers as far back as Socrates. Given the challenges you face from addictive digital devices, the twentieth-century teachers in this book will offer ways to engage your students face to face in a human community—a serious challenge. Letting your students know from the first day that you care about them and will listen to their lives will allow you to form close, trusted relationships. Essential for them—and for you as their teacher.

You will see how these teachers treat students as individuals. The classroom can become a sanctuary, the last vestige of hope where children can discover the joy of being together without intermediary devices. The last place to learn the value of body language and tone in conversations. Where gestures, animation, eye contact, and voice make for deeper understanding of one another. Human society began with people sitting around campfires having conversations. The classroom continues that tradition.

Paying attention to the conversations in *Listening Is Learning: Conversations between 20th and 21st Century Teachers*, which pair exemplary veterans with new teachers like yourself, will provide support and reassurance—not only from reading about them but will also encourage you to seek out your own conversations to grow as a teacher. Those who came before you, who exemplify best practices from another era, can become the foundation of your success.

You can't do it alone.

Acknowledgments

Teachers stand on the shoulders of countless others. The collection of people in my life is almost limitless. I am grateful for the plethora of gifts I've received in support of my teaching and writing.

Miss Karasack from grade school, Thomas Donovan from high school, Orville Murphy from college, and Reginald Archambault from graduate school. Del Goodwin, Barrie Rogers, Vin Rogers, and David Mallery, mentors. And may these few represent the many remarkable colleagues I've worked with over my forty years in the classroom: Terry Ortwein, Bill Murphy, Ford Daley, Bonnie Miller, Irina Nicholaevna, Raisa Vladimirovna, Winslow Myers, Mark Smith, Jane Crooks, Jan Cellucci, and countless others.

My consultant colleagues, notably Pat Karl, Bob Milley, Tony Polito, Jill Mirman, Rob Traver, Cheryl Bromley-Jones, Sue Freedman, John D'Auria, and Pamela Penna. And friends and readers, Hugh Silbaugh, Kathy Shepherd, Ursula Boyle, Rebecca Langrall, Dinty Moore, Ken Morrow, Chet Kozlowski, Rob Fried, Diana Spechler, David Ramsey, Gerald Helferich, and so many more who have critiqued and encouraged me.

My deep gratitude to administrators and office personnel, support staff including paraprofessionals, janitors, and cooks who made it possible every day for me to teach. And to those teachers who worked with me over my twelve years as a consultant.

And perhaps most important are my students throughout my nearly forty years in the classroom. Every day they were my teachers, my friends, my inspiration. Without them, I would not have been able to write this book.

Finally, I must acknowledge the wise and insightful counsel of the late Christina Ward who set me on the path to publish. She wisely shepherded me through the process. And the late Barbara Barnes, who as a friend and colleague for more than fifty years, believed in my teaching and writing. To Tom Koerner at Rowman & Littlefield who trusted me to make a difference to teachers. And a special appreciation to my wife, Kathleen Cammarata, whose art inspires me and whose words urge me to be honest with myself—and to my readers.

Frank Thoms
San Miguel de Allende, Mexico

Chapter 1

Break the Mold

Michael Harding and Meera Sharma

It was my show; I was holding a magic wand.

Michael Harding, white-haired, in his perennial bowtie, was reading his newspaper and drinking his cappuccino on Saturday morning at his favorite table at the Witney Café. He was in jeans, a brown sweater, and a black vest. He was reading the *New York Times* in print, at intervals smiling and frowning. He was waiting for Meera Sharma, new to the middle school social studies department at his former school.

She emailed him a few days ago asking if they could meet. She heard he was famous for his personal approach to the classroom. Already, she had been challenged with the impact of smartphones on the changing social landscape in her digitally driven twenty-first-century classroom. She wondered if Mr. Harding could provide guidance.

Meera had become aware of the devastating impact that personal screen time had in society. Sherry Turkle's seminal work, *Reclaiming Conversation: The Power of Talk in a Digital Age*,[1] had confirmed her concerns: "A quarter of American teenagers are connected to a device within five minutes of waking up. Most teenagers send one hundred texts a day. Eighty percent sleep with their phones. Forty-four percent do not 'unplug,' ever, not even in religious services or when playing a sport or exercising."[2]

Turkle's conclusions hit harder after Meera read Jean M. Twenge in *The Atlantic* about what Twenge calls iGen—the generation born between 1995 and 2012 that has been "shaped by the smartphone and the concomitant rise of social media."[3] They spend between six and eight hours a day on their phones. The smartphone has changed every aspect of their lives. They spend less time interacting socially. By consuming so much time alone they are, in Twenge's words, growing up slowly by not having social interactions with peers. And that's true in every household throughout the country. They live their lives on the phone, alone, in their room, on the bed—often distressed or depressed.

Thus, these children spend less time with one another. Twenge's conclusion was this: "Teens who spend more time than average on screen activities are more likely to be unhappy, and those who spend more time than average on non-screen activities are more likely to be happy. There's not a single exception. All screen activities are linked to less happiness, and all non-screen activities are linked to more happiness."[4] Meera reread these sentences several times.

That's why she emailed Mr. Harding. She figured that if she were to be effective, it would have to be separate from smartphones and away from screens. She'd already seen the effect of laptops in her own schooling; students surfed the web while pretending to listen to the teacher. In her student teaching, she watched at any given time as at least 20 percent of students attended to their smartphones. She was convinced she should base her classroom on eye contact, listening, interactions, and engagement. She would use digital technology—the school had carts with iPads—but only to serve her classroom's greater purpose.

"Good morning, Mr. Harding. I recognized your white hair and bowtie from across the room." Meera pulled out a chair, sat down, and slid off her jacket that covered her white, patterned blouse. She ran her fingers through her long brown hair, adjusted her red-rimmed glasses, and took out a notepad from her red pocketbook. She crossed her legs and dangled a red flat from her toes. She looked calm but apprehensive. How might a teacher from another time, before digitally distracted students, help her? She was eager to find out.

"Hello, Meera. Pleasure to meet you," putting out his right hand. "I am flattered that you want to ask me about teaching." Shifting in his seat, adjusting his green-striped suspenders, he smiled, "You probably know, Meera, I spent nearly forty years in the social studies department and ten more as a consultant before I retired. I wouldn't be surprised if remnants of my presence are still around."

"I'm sure they are judging from what I've heard from your fellow colleagues. I have so many questions; I'm not sure where to begin. Perhaps you could tell me how you became a teacher and what it was like for you when you started."

"Interesting you should ask, Meera. Now that I've let go of the daily routine—which I loved—I've been thinking about my path to teaching. I remember when I was ten or eleven, when I saw my father outside his office having a conversation with Jimmy Davidson, a "bum," as my friends—and everyone else it seemed—believed. For lack of a better term, we called him a "retard." He was squat, dressed in a tattered, flecked, dark wool suit, and had a speech defect. We would mock him behind his back.

"At home that evening, I asked my father why he would speak to Jimmy. 'Everyone is worth talking to, Michael, everyone.' He planted this thought, which I did not recognize at the time: that I should treat each person—and when I became a teacher, each student—as worth my time. I've not always followed my father's words, Meera, as I get caught up in paying special attention to 'important' people, but on a daily basis, the people in my life have not only been professors, teachers, students, shop owners, lawyers, and city officials but also postal clerks, garage attendants, janitors, cooks, waiters, street cleaners, and cab drivers. I know many of their names and their stories.

"By my sophomore year in college, I knew I'd become a teacher. I was lucky to choose teaching. I tell those who backed into the profession to choose to see it as a calling. They are there, in school, with colleagues, in their classroom, with students. They have taken a deep responsibility, perhaps deeper than at any time in our history, to be teachers, mentors, guides, and 'parents' to kids who are swimming in the chaos of social media. I envy you being there, and at the same time I'm glad for my turn of nearly fifty years.

"When students stepped into my first classroom, Meera, they brought who they were. No coffee-to-go in their hands. No smartphones. No buds in their ears. Eyes were on me, and they chatted with one another. They entered through a large oak door with frosted panes onto a creaky maple floor. They sat in five rows of metal-tubed desks with yellow laminate tops and bright-blue compartments, blue laminate chairs beneath—unlike in my school days when desks with inkwells were bolted to the floor.

"I loved that room," Mr. Harding said with a twinkle in his eye. "I can still see it: my teacher's oak desk with four deep drawers on each side and one in the center; a Roman numeral clock overhead encased in a brown, round, bevel-edged frame; behind, a blackboard with a tray having shards of white chalk and black felt erasers; above, an unrolled map; to the left an American flag; large multipaned windows on the far wall with pull-down tan shades; four hanging globed incandescent lights.

"To the right, a supply closet, door half-opened, showing dusty empty shelves: a dilapidated set of Carl Becker's *Modern History* at the top; below, a ream and a half of yellow-lined paper and a half ream of white-lined paper; a rubber-tipped chalkboard pointer resting in the corner—how strange it was to see this closet neglected compared to the pristine clean room. Inside the desk's wide center drawer, pieces of white chalk, a couple of wooden foot rulers, scattered paper clips, and not much else. I would need more paper, chalk, erasers, a stapler, paper clips, and purple ditto masters for making multiple copies—fundamental tools of my new trade."

"My room is not much different, Mr. Harding," Meera said. "I have a SMART board, but behind it is a green board with yellow chalk, a supply closet, armchair desks that are on wheels, fluorescent lights overhead, and two doors to the hallway. Desks in rows, my desk up front, a digital clock, and an American flag behind."

Meera was eager to hear about Mr. Harding's first year. He surprised her at how much he remembered. On his first day in homeroom, a boy with disheveled hair from the back asked, "Are you really our teacher, Mr. Harding? You look like a senior with a coat and tie."

"I tried to assure him, Meera, but the boy still appeared doubtful.

"That first year, I taught from a textbook energizing my classes in my brown tweed jacket, striped tie, khaki pants, and loafers employing humor, relentless questions, scribbles on the blackboard, and movement up and down the aisles. It was my show; I was holding a magic wand. I understood that I had the right, responsibility, and power to be in my ninth graders' lives, to affect their being, stimulate their thinking, and guide them to respect themselves in the world. I was blessed to be doing what I was called to do. No doubts at the time, but doubts would come. I was ready to take each day as a gift; a gift to me and a chance to give gifts to my students. I couldn't imagine what would be waiting in the wings."

Meera liked Mr. Harding's attitude. Being positive, energetic, and playful would be ideal. Yet she had to be sure to invoke good classroom management. Otherwise she would not have the opportunity to create an environment like his—and she would be facing distracted minds on their smartphones. Arriving at class, they would have just been on Snapchat, Instagram, or other apps—and probably texting as they walked in. To have their full attention, then, she would require them to put their shut-down phones into cubbies near the door.

Meera's conversation with Mr. Harding lasted more than two hours. They talked about material not discussed in her methods courses. He told her that he began that first year thinking he should treat students equally: have one deadline for assignments, give the same homework, offer only one type of test or quiz, and expect the same behavior. To choose to give some the benefit of the doubt would be unfair.

"But, Meera, one of my first students recently reminded me of our initial meeting. When she arrived a week after the opening of school, I gave her make-up assignments and prepared a make-up test. She did well but skipped one essay question, earning a B. I handed back her paper. She expressed disbelief, as she did not see the question.

"I hesitated, wondering if I should defy decorum and allow her a second chance. I did; she got an A. At the time I thought that was fair—and still do.

No child is like another, Meera. After all, we are not in a factory. We treat each student for who she is. We let them know we hear them, care about them."

Another point that Mr. Harding brought up was his early opposition to textbooks. At first, he used them to guide his curriculum; assigned homework at the end of each period, reviewed it first thing the next day, and, feeling like a master of ceremonies, asked most of the questions and fielded them before asking the next one. "But, Meera, I was doing what teachers did to me in school and how I learned how to teach in graduate school. It was the way I thought school should be."

"How did you break out of that paradigm?" Meera asked.

Mr. Harding paused. "Curious you should ask: I saw myself as one of a cadre of fellow liberal arts' graduates determined to set public education on its ear. As we prepared to become teachers, we hashed over the infamous James Conant report, *The American High School Today*.[5] We believed we knew better than teacher-college graduates—and believed that our profession was a noble calling. I saw us as a young elite bringing new energy into a tired system, being catalysts for learning, eager to do whatever we could to improve public education.

"But when I stepped into my classroom, the concept of cadre fell away. I committed to being unique and resolved to become the most creative teacher in the school. I've often thought why I chose to distinguish myself when all that was required was to implement the curriculum, use textbooks, make lesson plans, deliver knowledge, teach skills, give tests, and issue report cards. Had I done that, I certainly would have kept my contract.

"And I've thought a lot about seeds from my childhood. I made choices different from my friends, at least that's how I remember. I owned the only light-blue, three-speed Norman English bike among my friends' black Raleighs and Rudges. I was loyal to the Cleveland Indians amidst rabid Yankee and Red Sox fans. I threw a baseball right-handed but bowled with my left. I was the oldest son in a family that owned an inn, which had the biggest cellar in the neighborhood. And we had Studebakers. Perhaps my emphasis on those differences—as slight as they were—led me to see myself as different.

"As a result of my drive to be the best, Meera, I unwittingly bought into the protective-privacy culture of the classroom: the notion that whatever teachers do they keep close to the vest. I'm not proud of that. Had I'd been more open, other teachers could have seen what I was doing, and I might have seen what they were doing. We could have built a stronger camaraderie. The kids would have benefitted. I'm glad, Meera, that I eventually let go of having to be 'different' and sought to become more collegial.

"And my greatest fear in my first year," Mr. Harding said hesitantly, "was that I did not know enough. I dreaded questions to which I might not have known the answer. One day in late September, I was summarizing our unit on Napoleon Bonaparte—here's how I remember it." He sat up in his chair:

> "As you can see from our discussion, class, Napoleon was a cunning, skilled, clever general. He knew military tactics and could motivate his forces. His troops respected him. He was well prepared to win battles."
>
> "Was he driven to be who he was because he was compensating for being short?" interrupted Toni, my provocative student leaning back in her seat with a smirk on her face.
>
> "Being short? What difference could that make?" I asked, probably appearing nervous tapping my fingers (uh-oh, I'm in trouble!).
>
> "Well, think about it, Mr. Harding. Being short may have pushed Napoleon to overcompensate. I thought you would know that. And what do you know about the paintings where he kept his right hand in his vest?" (What *do* I know about that?)
>
> "That's a good question, Toni," (and deflecting her query), "What does anyone else think?"

"Toni was one of my most precocious—and tallest. Others pointed out what I thought I could have known—or probably should have. After all, I was the one up front—the one who should know everything about his subject. To compensate for my fear, I became a tough grader. It would provide cover from anyone discovering that I'd earned no A's in college. But that did not last. After the first marking period, the guidance counselor called me into his office.

"Sitting behind his desk, peering over his spectacles, and in a firm voice, he said, 'You have only five A's, fifteen B's, seventeen C's, thirty-five D's, and seven F's. You have way too many D's and F's, Michael! Your bell curve is slanted too far to the left. We can't tolerate that.'

"There went my plan to be a tough grader! Besides it was not a good idea."

Their time was up at the café. Meera thanked Mr. Harding for sharing his wisdom. She asked if they could meet again. Mr. Harding suggested a month from now to give Meera time to settle in.

Mr. Harding was flattered that a young colleague was eager to hear from him. He wondered how she perceived his childhood stories. He wondered, too, if she'd think his methods might be perceived as outmoded. And he wondered how Meera heard about his early desire to be a unique teacher. Most of his colleagues had followed traditional methodologies and talked or lectured from the front of the room. Yet, he had no hesitation to be himself, to want to be his kind of teacher. "I hope I can make that clear the next time Meera and I meet," he said to himself.

And he'd known about Sherry Turkle and Jean M. Twenge's research on screens and had felt distant from his grandchildren when they were with him on their devices. He sensed that were he to reenter the classroom, he would stay clear of smartphones, laptops, and tablets, at least most of the time. One of his great joys in the classroom was the endless conversations, especially the open-ended kind.

As Meera left the café that morning, she was buzzing with ideas. She realized she could stand on the shoulders of a former teacher. Mr. Harding had been away from the classroom for twenty years, but she was learning from him—and probably would from other twentieth-century teachers; her conversation had her rethinking her reasons for becoming a teacher. She may be a teacher in the digital age, but she, too, will be with children—human beings wanting to understand themselves in the world.

In the course of their Saturday conversation, Mr. Harding told Meera that he put his desks into a horseshoe in the spring of his first year—and it shifted his perception of teaching. As much as he loved "the show"—standing at the front, in charge—he now had livelier discussions, more student insights, more learning. His students saw him as a person who knew them well, better perhaps than their parents. At the beginning of her second week, Meera rearranged her desks into a two-layered horseshoe to accommodate her classes of up to twenty-nine students:

> "Whoa, Ms. Sharma! Why don't you keep the desks in rows like all the other teachers? Why have you put them this way?" asked David, who indicated that he liked sitting in his usual seat at the front.
> "If you'll just take a seat, any seat, David, you'll find out."
> When everyone was in the room, Ms. Sharma asked for quiet. "Now that you're all here, you see that the desks are arranged into two horseshoes. Any idea why?"
> Bonnie from her homeroom raised her hand. "You want us to talk more to each other? You want us . . . to interact more?"
> "Yes, that's exactly the reason. You will see each other's faces, as well as mine. Ms. Sharma will sit here at the open-end. We will be able to have conversations."
> "Yes, but you are the one who's supposed to teach us stuff, Ms. Sharma," said Peter, who was eager to pay attention. "How will we learn from talking to each other?"
> "You'll soon find out, Peter."

At first, they had difficulty looking at each other and talking. Meera attributed it to their preference for texting. She'd seen groups sitting at tables, texting rather than talking. Even when walking, they would text. But she was determined to have them become conversationalists. She decided to ask for Mr. Harding's advice on this topic next month at the café.

NOTES

1. Sherry Turkle, *Reclaiming Conversation: The Power of Talk in a Digital Age* (New York: Penguin Press, 2015).

2. Ibid., 42.

3. Jean M. Twenge, "Have Smartphones Destroyed a Generation?" *The Atlantic*, September 2017.

4. Ibid.

5. James Conant, *The American High School Today: A First Report to Interested Citizens* (New York: McGraw-Hill, 1959).

Chapter 2

Engage Students

Michael Harding and Meera Sharma

Listen up, kids! The United States should build a dam from Florida to Cuba to blockade the Gulf Stream!

Mr. Harding was reading editorials and drinking a cappuccino at his regular table. Hardly saying hello, Meera sat down with her tea and barely taking a breath, began, "I followed your advice and put my desks in a horseshoe, Mr. Harding, but my kids hesitated to look each other in the eye and talk. They sit, fidget, hardly look at each other—and miss their phones."

"Putting my desks in a horseshoe was not a simple decision," said Mr. Harding. "No one else was doing it—and I was only in my first year. Before I tell you more about my early years teaching, Meera, I want to share with you some of the thoughts I had before stepping into my classroom the first day. Let me read a journal account I wrote":

Who is this young man standing before his unsuspecting students? I was there because I'd found my calling; I wanted to teach. But I was also that person who, at ten years old, was put in a corner by his neighbor, Mrs. Henderson, after she slapped the back of my hand with a hairbrush for misbehaving in her house. I was that college student, a good athlete, who nearly flunked out in his sophomore year. Who was I to think I was to be a teacher, to be a role model for adolescents?

My first jobs as a newspaper boy and soda jerk taught me the value of doing work well. And other memories had their impact. On a day when my mother invited guests to our home, she caught me—at four-years-old—standing naked at the door: "Hi, I'm Mikey Harding. Come in! Come in!" Embarrassed as she must have been, I think I'm lucky to still have that exuberance. And—not so positive—I recall my mother sending me more than once from the dining table to my room. Will I do something wrong with my students and be sent to the principal's office?

I came to public school from the upside of town but befriended those from the lower side. I learned—unbeknownst at the time—that every person counts. And before my first day with my new students, I understand that each one of them is on his own path becoming his unique self. After all, I am becoming who I am.

"As I told you, Meera," Mr. Harding continued, "I did not put my desks into a horseshoe until the spring. I was too taken by being the master of ceremonies. Imagine me in my first year: After the bell would ring, I closed my door. I was in charge. Kids were looking up at me. I initiated lessons; spoke fast; asked provocative questions; elaborated on each answer, hardly waiting before asking the next question; scribbled on the blackboard; and invoked humor, especially puns. I never sat at my desk except for when I gave a quiz or test. I was an entertainer advocating for excitement in history.

"In fact, punning became one of my mantras," said Mr. Harding. "They flowed seamlessly from the context of our conversations, so many that I hardly recall them—fleeting moments they were. One of my favorites involved my Doc Martens. One day I suddenly stopped teaching, looked down, astonished, and said, 'Oh my God, kids, I can't believe it. I've had these shoes for a year and never realized: I'm in a paradox!' You can imagine the chuckles—especially mine. Yet, as I look back, I wonder sometimes if puns interrupted the flow of conversation. I hoped not, but I'm not sure."

"It sounds like, Mr. Harding," said Meera, "that you plunged into teaching, and despite doubts, held nothing back. My path has been different but no less a commitment. That's why, as I said earlier, I'm perplexed at the lack of response from my kids. They seem to lack curiosity, something I and my friends exuded at their age."

"That's a tough issue, Meera. As you might imagine, I never had such distractions," Mr. Harding said in a quiet voice. "My first suggestion, from an old teacher, is for you is to let your students know you want to know them. By listening, they see you as one who cares. Next, look for engaging material—outside the textbook—in hopes of drawing students in and enticing them to express their opinions. I had latitude in deciding curriculum and methods and did not have the pressure you have to meet standards and respond to outside tests. For instance, for my unit on Soviet Russia, I chose to abandon the textbook and use George Orwell's classic, *Animal Farm*."

"One of my favorite books," Meera said wide-eyed.

"I made the conscious decision, Meera," Mr. Harding stressed, "not to tell them anything about Orwell, the background to the book, its purpose, and its Soviet connection. I put the book in their hands for them to discover its meaning. *Animal Farm* would be theirs. I assigned one chapter at a time—no one was to read ahead—and I prepared a study guide. Class discussions became a search for understanding each chapter as the story evolved. Among the most memorable conversations focused on how the dogs were able to drive Snowball, the white pig, off the farm. My contention: Snowball's culpability for his own demise; had he been wise, he would have seen it coming!

"Evidence for my contention emerged: Napoleon taking puppies up to the loft; his absence from the Battle of the Cowshed; his peeing on Snowball's plans for the windmill; Snowball's superfluous committees; and his diminishing the seven commandments to 'Four Legs Good, Two Legs Bad.' Other discussions focused on whether the drunk Mr. Jones was a good farmer, what the pigs contributed to the farm, what the hens gave up when smashing their eggs, and the pigs' involvement with whiskey."

Knowing the book well, Meera could imagine the discussions.

"Let me tell one more happening with *Animal Farm*. I'd just received an Apple desk computer for my classroom, which tempted me to become more creative. Besides making documents, I played with them. For one, I put 'Pigs rule' in nine-point Helvetica font in the footer. I wanted to set a tone. And for my abridgment of the *Communist Manifesto*, I put at the bottom of the fourth page." He showed Meera:

Abridged by Comrade Mikhail Mikhailovich Harding
for the education of the emerging elite
of the excellent Eighth Echelon
who absorb knowledge & wisdom
in Party Cell 311

"In addition, I had a collection of rubber stamps: dancing pigs, a smirking front-facing pig, among others—and one of a pig's rear end. When passing back quizzes and homework, I would choose a stamp to reflect the quality of the work: the dancing pigs for excellence, and the pig's rear end for not-so-good—and because I liked to use it, I took every opportunity to be playful because it fostered good relationships, and it helped make teaching fun."

"What I'm gleaning, Mr. Harding, is that you put yourself into your classroom," Meera said with a smile. "You invited your students to become immersed. It became a personal experience for all of you. Not a delivery process; it was yours—and became theirs!"

"Thank you, Meera. I appreciate your insights. Shortly after I taught *Animal Farm* for the first time, I came up with a metaphor. I'd seen so many teachers—mine included—presenting themselves as information providers. Putting my students into the mix with Orwell and his animals showed me a much better way. I was perhaps more grateful than my students.

"Here is the metaphor I came up with." He handed her a copy. "We can begin to envision ourselves as giving piano lessons. We are the piano teacher who invites her student to play alongside, provides steady feedback and then sends him home to practice his newfound skills. If, on the other hand, she were to have her student watch as she demonstrated how the keys moved, how the notes played, pointed to the score, and so on, her student would leave without any techniques and skills with which to practice."

"This metaphor illustrates," Mr. Harding emphasized, "that teachers are responsible for making learning happen *in the classroom*. It's not enough to assume that what we tell students they will learn at home. Some children do not have support, let alone a place to work. Besides it's not right. I found that the more learning that occurs in the classroom, the more learning happens."

"I love this metaphor, Mr. Harding," Meera said. "So simple. So direct. I had piano lessons and was fortunate that my teacher had me play for her—and with her. I'm going to put 'teachers are responsible for making learning happen *in the classroom*' on my computer to remind me to think of teaching as doing, doing the learning. And to prompt me to build strong relationships."

For the next half hour Meera and Mr. Harding elucidated their understandings of *Animal Farm* and other classics including *1984* and William Golding's *Lord of the Flies*. Meera was fascinated with Mr. Harding's account on bringing Orwell into his classroom. But she would not have the space and time to include *Animal Farm* in her curriculum—at least not now.

Realizing her situation, Mr. Harding suggested a shorter provocation. "Read aloud James Clavell's *The Children's Story*[1] and open it up for discussion. It would take a day or two—and longer if you wanted to.

"Written during the Cold War, it's the chilling tale of primary school children being brainwashed: The new teacher has them question the pledge of allegiance, to cut up the flag so each child could have a piece, to toss the flagpole out the window with glee, to wear uniforms, to agree to stay overnight with this new teacher, to close their eyes to pray to their Leader rather than to God, *and* to agree to keep secrets from their parents—all in the span of twenty-five minutes."

Although the Soviet Union wasn't in her curriculum, Meera was determined to use Clavell; she would provide some background before reading it aloud—and it might open the door for them to engage in conversation.

After an hour, Mr. Harding had to leave. Meera thanked him for his ideas, particularly for *The Children's Story*. As he was walking out of the café, Michael Harding thought back to moments in his early years. He recalled his struggle, so different from Meera's, of having to teach tracked classes: students placed in four levels from the fourth grade. As a young teacher, he saw top sections as bright, college material; middle sections on the verge of success if they were willing to work; and the bottom sections, most of whom came from the edge of town, likely to remain there after high school. Except for advanced math and AP courses in her school, Meera would not teach tracked sections.

Two memories about this system have stuck with him: The first was his freewheeling conversation with one of his top sections during their study of U.S.–Soviet relations. He practically remembers it word-for-word:

> "Listen up, kids! The United States should build a dam from Florida to Cuba to blockade the Gulf Stream! This dam will divert warm waters from reaching the Baltic Sea, which would immerse the western Soviet Union into a deep freeze. What do you guys think of this idea?"
>
> Everyone looked at one another. One said, "You're crazy, Mr. Harding. You can't build a dam that big, especially in the ocean! No way!"
>
> "Yea, that's right," said another. "Besides, Cuba is Russia's ally and would not put up with it!"
>
> "And," another shouted, "what will happen to the temperature in Great Britain, in Europe—and in New England? President Johnson would never consider doing that!"

An absurd moment, Michael Harding reminded himself with a broad smile. One of the joys of being a teacher! A Florida–Cuba dam? Certainly not! But nevertheless, a lively conversation: provocative, creative, colorful—and messy. He recollected, "One reason I loved what I was doing! I remember pulling down my eight-foot-tall, Denoyer-Geppert polar-projection map of the northern hemisphere, which covered the blackboard. Students jumped at the chance to challenge my argument—and from what they said the next day, they continued having dinner conversations with their parents! The best kind of homework! Meera would enjoy hearing about this."

But a second and more serious memory, Michael Harding thought to himself, concerned tracking, which happened during his second year: He was projecting to his lowest section a rented black-and-white film on farming in Latin America. He was running it backward——he wasn't supposed to as he'd been told that it would widen the sprockets. His kids were laughing as they watched a farmer un-eating his banana when the school secretary burst into the room to tell them that President Kennedy had been shot. Shot!

"What did I think I was doing?" he thought. "Projecting a film backwards—and at this moment! I was treating these kids as less capable, less bright, and less teachable. I was thinking they were not potential learners, thinking I'd have to pull teeth to get them to learn anything! I needed to be better than that. When I look back, I should have been ashamed of my behavior.

"But I was in a culture that separated people: at the top, smart; in the middle, possibly smart; at the bottom, no chance. I believed that. A few years later, a former student said that I determined in the first week who were the smart ones in the class. I was shocked and from that moment I decided to find potential in everyone and nurture it. Teaching became more about them.

"I wonder what Meera will think of these stories."

Meanwhile Meera left their conversation hopeful that she could engage her students' curiosity and get them to look at one another and discuss. She couldn't wait to read aloud Clavell's *The Children's Story*—twice if she had to—and wait for them to start talking. It would be a long haul for them to feel that Ms. Sharma's classroom was their home away from home. She would persist. "This is the right path," she said to herself.

The day to read Clavell came. Meera was so surprised at her success that she sent Mr. Harding an email. She wrote that Clavell's story astonished her students:

> "That could never happen, Ms. Sharma, never, you know it couldn't!"
> "How could a young stranger take over from their teacher?"
> "We'd never let our teacher be sent to the office by someone we don't know."
> "I never got a dime for saying the pledge!"

Meera concluded the email with her insight that she shared that day:

> How, then, can you expect the children in this story not to be captivated by a beautiful, young, proper, pretty, perfumed person dressed in olive-green clothes and wearing olive-green shoes, who sits on the floor and sings to them, who replaces their gray-haired teacher with old eyes and well-worn clothes? And why wouldn't they want a piece of the flag? And keeping secrets from their parents—how cool is that!

Meera and Mr. Harding stayed in touch throughout the year, meeting at least once a month. She was grateful that he became her mentor. She did not know what she would have done without him.

NOTE

1. James Clavell, *The Children's Story* (New York: Delacorte Press, 1963).

Chapter 3

Invoke Primary Sources

Frances Smith and Joyce Bertrand

Without self, there are no others, and without others, there is no self.

Meera Sharma told Joyce Bertrand, a fellow new teacher, about her two visits with Mr. Harding. She suggested that Joyce—curious, bright, and excited to be a teacher—reach out to Frances Smith, also retired from the school. Mrs. Smith was well known for her innovative curriculum on Chinese history and philosophy, a course to which Joyce was assigned. They arranged to meet at the same place Mr. Harding and Meera met, the Witney Café.

Frances Smith, with white hair and rimless glasses and a restless demeanor, looked like a scholar. She appeared relaxed but reflected an eagerness to talk. Joyce spotted her at the back of the café. As she approached she introduced herself with zest, vigor, and a hopeful attitude, something Mrs. Smith immediately saw. They shook hands as Joyce sat down. She came prepared with many questions. Mrs. Smith briefly told Joyce about her thirty-five years of teaching the eighth grade. And yes, she confirmed she was known for her unique approaches to China.

For the next hour, they became engrossed.

"What you teach is up to you, Joyce, and don't let anyone tell you different. I know you are faced with pressures to meet standards, to prepare for outside testing, but let me tell you, we had our pressures. We believed that we were to teach the same way everyone else was teaching: to stand at the front of the room, deliver information, and find out if students got it. It's the way I went to school and how I was taught.

"By the end of my first year, I saw that the emperor was not wearing any clothes. I delivered my lessons, kids took notes (at least some of them), and I gave tests: a few got A's, some B's, mostly C's, and inevitably some F's. No matter how I delivered, the same pattern. In essence, I was sorting them out and indicating their future.

"But, I asked myself this: Isn't school supposed to be a place where everyone learns, where everyone succeeds? In the early industrial revolution, schools were sorting institutions designed like factories. They sent most pupils to work; the few who succeeded went to better jobs. But that doesn't cut it, Joyce, not anymore.

"I decided that I would teach for learning and not to try impress kids with what I knew. I wanted to see them learn in front of me, not send them home to answer questions at the end of a chapter or study their notes. I will say, however, that I'm intrigued with the notion of the flipped classroom, exemplified by Khan Academy: to study new material online at home and come to class to process it.[1] I would certainly include this approach today. I want to tell you, Joyce, how I brought learning front and center when teaching ancient Chinese thought late in my career."

Mrs. Smith leaned back slightly and raised her eyebrows. "The textbook on China only provided descriptions of what was otherwise fascinating. It made brief references to Chinese thought, my favorite topic. I tried at first to make the textbook work but to no avail; it lacked narrative. Once my students had a good idea of the geography of China and its early history, I abandoned it.

"For the unit on Confucius, the first day I passed out Confucian analects without comment. I could have chosen to explain Confucian philosophy, interpreted the analects, and given a test, but that was not my intention. Without any explanation I decided to put analects before them and listen. Here are two." Mrs. Smith handed Joyce a copy:

> Confucius said, "In serving his parents, a son may gently remonstrate with them. When he sees that they are not inclined to listen to him, he should resume an attitude of reverence and not abandon his effort to serve them. He may feel worried but does not complain." (4:18)
>
> The Duke of She told Confucius, "In my country there is an upright man named Kung. When his father stole a sheep, he bore witness against him." Confucius said, "The upright men in my community are different from this. The father conceals the misconduct of his son, and the son conceals the misconduct of his father. Uprightness is found in this." (13:18)[2]

"These examples of Confucian filial piety tested my students. Some questioned Confucius's advising a son to 'remonstrate'—they loved that word—and to have 'reverence' when they thought they were right and their father wrong. I hesitated to jump into the conversations. Had I, I might not have heard the wisdom of Alexis, one of my wisest students, who attributed the turning in of one's father to her understanding of the story of the Soviet,

Pavlov Morozov, who informed on his father and was then shot by the authorities, or from Adam, another thoughtful student: 'When a son reveals the misconduct of his father, he destroys the fabric of his family. If it happens in many other families, society could dissolve.' I've never forgotten comments like these."

Joyce then asked how she evaluated her students' understanding of Confucian thought—particularly what kind of test did she give. Mrs. Smith smiled.

"I did not give quizzes or tests. I gave writing assignments. At the time, I'd never considered teaching Chinese history but was assigned to it. I was hesitant, but I remembered Shunryu Suzuki's wise words: 'In the beginner's mind there are many possibilities, but in the expert's, there are few.'[3] I didn't have to know or pretend to know. I saw myself as a teacher, and my students as teachers."

The Suzuki quotation resonated with Joyce. She saw herself in her classroom with students different from who she was at their age. She and her classmates had come to school with little comparative baggage; some had problems at home, others were anxious about peer relationships, but not much else. Joyce now watched her kids enter her room distracted, disinterested, and unwilling—and unable—to become involved. They knew much more than she did at their age—information overload—but it seems to cause them anxiety. Mrs. Smith's approach to Confucius was opening her eyes.

One year, instead of giving a test, Mrs. Smith told Joyce she published a blue-cover booklet of her students' seventy-six analects: *The Wisdom of Confucius: As Written and Understood by Her Devoted Disciples, under the Tutelage of Frances-Shi*. She gave each one a Chinese name; she showed Joyce six examples.

> Josh-lu, devoted disciple of Confucius, asked, "Which is more important, self or others?" Confucius replied, "Without self, there are no others and without others there is no self." (2:8)
>
> Bak-alt, who likes to speak in one liners, was found speaking to some children in the village: "Do not criticize others if you yourself cannot do better. Do not daydream but be attentive and learn your lessons. Play as a unit, not as an individual. And respect your elders!" The children were in awe. (3:3)
>
> Cait-lin, a whimsical disciple of Confucius who loved to run in the woods, quipped, "In a race it is more fun to beat the boys than draw hearts around their names." (3:4)
>
> Liss-Di, reflecting her devotion to Confucius while tapping her toes in the wind, said, "When you see a stranger in pain and spring into action, you show respect for others. If you sit and watch, you are selective and disrespectful." (4:12)

> As Sean-Ginn, a devoted disciple of Confucius wrote, "Listen to those who talk to you and you in turn will be heard." (2:3)
>
> In reflecting the wisdom of Confucius, Dor-si, a devoted and reverent follower, said, "Kindness is like a stream of water. It makes rough tough rocks smooth." Confucius rode on with a broad smile on his face.

Joyce Bertrand wished she had learned about Confucius in this way. "I can see from their analects that your students 'got' Confucius. Primary sources have the obvious potential to engage thinking, and I now see that they can encourage kids to generate 'new' primary sources! This is much better than having to learn from a dry textbook. I will have to find ways to generate this type of assignment. And maybe I could incorporate the iPad where they could interact as they devise documents. So much better than being alone on screens; they might come to like it! Once done, they could read to each other, invite questions, and get suggestions. It would be using a familiar tool but would move them toward interaction. Before we're done, I would have them to put away the iPads and discuss their impressions."

"I like your way of thinking, Joyce! A great habit for all teachers! After Confucius, I used a similar approach with Lao Tzu's *Tao Te Ching*. I selected from its eighty-one chapters several for them to ponder, again choosing to sit back and listen.

"And because I was free to design curriculum, I assigned Benjamin Hoff's *The Tao of Pooh*. Hoff's dialogues with Pooh opened my thirteen-year-olds to Lao Tzu's mind: *Wu Wei*, doing without doing, causing, or making; 'Things Are as They Are,' where everything has its own place and function; accepting one's 'Inner Nature,' to be oneself; contemplating the 'Uncarved Block,' seeing things in their natural state; and weighing the 'Tiddely-Pom Principle,' where respect builds 'Respect.'

"The combination of *Tao* chapters and the whimsy of Taoist Winnie the Pooh and his Hundred Acre friends, Joyce, brought home this intriguing philosophy." Mrs. Smith handed Joyce the directions for an assignment at the end of the unit with examples and asked Joyce to read it aloud:

> Find your way into the Tao; your way to understand it. Tap into the deeper recesses of your mind and heart. You've explored a selection of Taoist chapters, Chuang-tzu's crooked tree and man bobbing in turbulent water, Thich Nhat Hanh's pirate and the girl, and the simplicity of Pooh. Share what you understand. Write your own Taoist aphorisms:

> As it is said in the *Tao Te Ching*, you must discover yourself before you can go out and change the world. (Matt)
>
> Look at what we have, and what we've accomplished. Then find happiness in this. (Rachel)

By being ourselves we can form our own character and personality. If we are always wishing to be something other than what we are, we will never know what we want out of life. (Gina)

We can flow to the end of the year as a river, moving around obstacles, having our effect on our surroundings and not minding if things don't go as expected. (Sarah)

Those who do not stop and smell the roses will soon have none to smell. If you do not appreciate the good things you do and that are given to you, they will no longer be there. (Tod)

"I posted these aphorisms in large lettering above the lockers in the hall outside my room. I wanted their work to be recognized and to intrigue future eighth graders. I made it public to invite others to recognize their efforts. After all, drama and music departments go public with their performances!" Joyce liked this idea.

"I used a different approach to introduce the Buddha, Joyce, the third way of thought in ancient China. Mixing up methodologies kept my classroom alive. Here's the introductory quotation I used from Charlotte Joko Beck":

> We are rather like whirlpools in the river of life. In flowing forward, a river or stream may hit rocks, branches, or irregularities in the ground, causing whirlpools to spring up spontaneously here and there. . . . The stability of a whirlpool is only temporary. The energy of the river of life forms living things—a human being, a cat or dog, trees and plants—then what held the whirlpool in place is itself altered, and the whirlpool is swept away, reentering the larger flow. The energy that was a particular whirlpool fades out and the water passes on, perhaps to be caught again and turned for a moment into another whirlpool.[4]

"Beck's whirlpool metaphor illustrates two key Buddhist principles: impermanence and reincarnation. I followed with writings of contemporary Buddhists: the Dalai Lama, Thich Nhat Hanh, Bhikkhu Bodhi, Sylvia Boorstein, Steve Hagen, and Beck. By the end of the unit, my students understood what it meant to follow the Buddha's example of how to live: First, take refuge in the Dharma. Next, step on the path to freedom, and last, join a Sangha, the community of fellow practitioners who guide, support, and befriend. And we were forming our own Sangha."

"OK," Joyce said leaning forward, "you had them write their own analects, had them write Taoist sayings that you posted, and ostensibly set up their own Sangha. Did you give them a final test?"

"No, Joyce, I'm glad you asked. Late at night, sitting at my computer, I had an epiphany. I came up with an invitation to my students to search ancient wisdom: 'Your mission is to discover your own understanding of what matters and to use your understanding to serve the greater good.'

"And here's an excerpt of the eight-page document with specific instructions, which I wrote that night entitled, 'A Modern Fable: Searching for the Three Great Ways.' I think this approach might intrigue you."

> A community had the habit of gathering once a month to discuss the meaning of life. Affectionately called "The Meeting," members practiced meditative conversation to seek the guidance of the inner spirit. They would speak only when called. The purpose of the spoken word was to minister to the group. No person was the leader. Because of the community's success, people from far and wide came there to live. As years passed, the community became overwhelmed, more diverse, and less coherent.
>
> One day Sister Carolyn arose. "We have become different from who we once were. We need to seek help to recover the harmony, love, and acceptance with one another that has been our hallmark. I understand in the land of ancient China there are Three Great Ways of thought that guide their people. Their wisdom might help recover our sense of community."
>
> Brother Christopher arose. "I have heard Sister Carolyn's words. I suggest that we send our brightest young people to ancient China and bring back knowledge of the Three Great Ways. The young, after all, best understand the movement of the spirit and can bring it to us."
>
> After much discussion, Sister Carolyn again stood. "May the young who venture on this journey be guided by the spirit of love and compassion to serve. May they find answers from the Three Great Ways that will nurture our beloved community."
>
> Teacher Frances arose. The community knew her as an older teacher who knew the ways of the young and who had their best interests at heart. Many had learned from her when they, too, were young. Though her hair had turned white and her skin more wrinkled, they knew her as a kind teacher. Teacher Frances professed to the community, "As you know, I have a deep love for the Three Great Ways. May I be allowed to guide the young on their journey? The best way for them to serve will be for them to search for the meaning of the Three Great Ways. Only then will they be able to serve well. I've prepared four questions from which to choose to guide their search":
>
>> How am I to understand and better myself?
>> How am I to live within my family so peace and harmony prevail?
>> How am I to relate to others so goodness prevails?
>> How am I to live well within nature and the environment?

"This scenario, Joyce, combined with the four questions provided doorways into the Three Great Ways. My students were to write a personal statement, to dwell within themselves, discover their own truths using sources we discussed in class; no further research necessary. The document instructed them how to cite evidence, structure their papers, how they'd be evaluated, and gave writing samples and due dates. I'd be glad to give you a copy if you'd like.

"As a result, many saw themselves in a new light, often with astonishment. The papers reflected the generosity of the assignment. Here are a few of my students' comments":

> I thought I knew myself before writing this paper, but now I understand myself differently and more clearly. Thank you, Mrs. Smith. (Dorsy)
>
> Completing this assignment was one of the most satisfying things I've ever done.... I became enlightened. (John)
>
> I learned a lot about leadership. I learned not to take leadership for power or for privilege but to lead when called upon. (Sam)
>
> This kind of paper actually had importance in my life. During the past few weeks, I found myself saying, "Would a Taoist have done that?" The answer was always "No." And I sometimes quoted Confucius when an issue came up in my family. (Paul)

"These were but four of the nearly fifty expressions of appreciation—more than appreciation. The four questions, while setting parameters, allowed for a rare personal freedom. If I may say, the search for ancient wisdom succeeded, because it

- tapped into core human concerns;
- evoked passion for seeking wisdom and relating it to their lives;
- put fundamental human qualities at the forefront, including civility, kindness, generosity, gratitude, helpfulness, self-awareness, competence, hope, truth, wisdom, engagement, respect, responsibility, care, compassion, communication, and empathy; and
- demanded rigorous reading and rereading, writing and rewriting, and probing—and engendered a sense that we were in this search together.

"My cherubs tapped into newfound insights—their interior landscapes—as they wrote about seeking universal truths inherent in the questions. While some struggled to grasp the implications of their discoveries, all of them pushed the envelope. I am grateful I asked. I think, too, that this project succeeded because my students and I had a close relationship. They knew I wanted to hear from them—their thinking, feelings—and not what they thought I would want to hear. I hope, Joyce, you will find a way to create this experience for your kids. I have given you a lot to ponder, but I did not want to shortchange what became an important teaching paradigm for me.

"Years later a student wrote me a letter that I want to share with you." She read an excerpt:

You asked us to use the wisdom of the three ways of thought from ancient China to guide our own lives on the path to goodness and morality. Never before have I been implored to answer such a personal question and define my beliefs. You gave this exercise to show the way into young adulthood, to prevent my classmates and me from compromising our beliefs before we defined them.

You designed it to help us become emotionally and spiritually ready for the next chapter of our lives. You instituted the most important composition we have had to complete thus far.

"Good teaching, after all, demands commitment, preparation, and persistence. It means to offer students the room to seek truth, to find what matters to their souls. Cookie-cutter curriculums curtail the mind, the heart. Nothing worthwhile comes easy. And for you, Joyce, pulling kids away from the shallow processing of their phones may be doubly difficult, but don't give up. We need people who can think, who can persist to meet challenges. Ask a lot, stick with it, and you and your students will be rewarded. Nothing satisfies more than struggling to get to a worthwhile end, and that end becomes a beginning."

Joyce was overwhelmed with her conversation with Mrs. Smith. Her curriculum was designed to meet end-of-the-year standardized tests, an issue Mrs. Smith didn't face. The department expected Joyce to use the world history textbook from which she would cover China and other non-Western topics. How, then, was she going to dig as deep as Mrs. Smith had? She recalled Shunryu Suzuki's, "In the beginner's mind there are many possibilities, but in the expert's, there are few." Joyce thought, "I may not know not what I need to know, but I can get there!"

However, only a few weeks into the school year, Joyce saw her students' frustrations with the textbook. Not only was it difficult to comprehend, but also it was heavy to carry. Perhaps she could use the iPad carts to lessen the burden. Joyce decided she would bring up her concerns at the next department meeting. However, she did not have much hope.

Meanwhile, she would take incremental steps to incorporate some of Mrs. Smith's approaches. When introducing China, she would have the textbook explain the geography and early history, but she would add maps and images from other sources on her SMART board to enrich the conversation. Then she would take two days—not enough but a beginning—using the iPads to present Confucian analects. She wanted to see how well her students would engage in interpreting them. However, she anticipated their struggle to take responsibility for expressing their understanding, but having conversations would be worth the effort.

Mrs. Smith smiled as Joyce headed out of the café. She saw herself in her protégé. She, too, had been on her own from her first day. She'd been assigned textbooks to use for her tracked sections: a college-level text for the top groups and Carl Becker's *Modern History* for the others. It took her awhile to see that the textbooks weren't cutting it. On parents' night she gave a handout to let them know her stance (she would show it to Joyce next time):

> Teaching for me is life. The life process comes alive in the classroom. Here I engage with the minds of those with whom I have been entrusted. . . . I feel that whatever I teach must be on the edge of what I know.
>
> Texts can serve to open life to all of us. A textbook, on the other hand, often loses vitality because it speaks down without encouraging thoughts to come to it. It does the thinking for the students; it asks for regurgitation. Regurgitation, like milk, is for cows.

Fortunately, Frances Smith taught in a time and in a school where she could decide her curricula. Within a year, textbooks had taken a backseat in her classroom, relegated to the closet.

NOTES

1. https://www.khanacademy.org.
2. "Confucius, the Teacher and Person," Columbia East Asian Institute, 1994; today this material can be found at Asia for Educators at Columbia (afe.easia.columbia.edu).
3. Shunryu Suzuki, *Zen Mind, Beginner's Mind* (New York: Weatherhill, 1970), 21.
4. Charlotte Joko Beck, *Nothing Special: Living Zen* (New York: HarperCollins, 1994), 3.

Chapter 4

Frame the Big Picture

Michael Harding, Frances Smith, Meera Sharma, and Joyce Bertrand

Coca-Cola is everywhere.

After her meeting with Mrs. Smith, Joyce called Meera to thank her. In the course of their conversation, Meera suggested that they both meet with Mr. Harding and Mrs. Smith. "Who knows what we will discover? Who knows!"

The following Saturday after lunch they found the veterans sitting at a corner table at the Witney Café. Meera introduced Joyce to Mr. Harding. They ordered coffees, except Meera who ordered chai tea. After having recalled their separate meetings with their protégés, Mrs. Smith and Mr. Harding agreed that they would talk about the importance of an often-neglected principle for the classroom: framing the big picture.

"When teachers rely on the sequence of chapters in a textbook to determine curriculum, students have little idea where they are going," said Mr. Harding. "They can't see the end of the road—and are often surprised when they get there. And the title of a course hardly indicates its contents. 'American history 1776–1865' doesn't say much.

"More than twenty-five years ago at a workshop, I learned about an idea I've kept in the forefront of my mind. Fred Jervis, president of the Center for Constructive Change, asked, 'What is an ideal doorman?' We offered a litany of qualities: 'appears well-dressed,' 'holds the door,' 'smiles,' 'is efficient,' 'carries bags,' 'hails cabs,' 'knows the neighborhood restaurants and their menus.' . . . Fred then let us know where he was taking us: 'Once you know the characteristics of an ideal doorman and you want to become one, you can plan backwards to get yourself there.'

"He was so profound! It was the first time I understood the power of an end in view. You never know, Meera and Joyce, where you'll find good ideas.

At another workshop many years later, a consultant shared another approach, which I've revised." Mr. Harding handed out copies.

> It's the day before the opening of school. You've not met your new students. Now step back and visualize yourself standing outside your door as if it were the last day. See them leaving. They will no longer be yours. You ask yourself such questions as these:
>
>> Who are they now that they've been in my class for the year?
>> What have they learned?
>> How do they think?
>> How do they relate to the world? To each other?
>> What do they understand about themselves?
>> What is most important to them?
>> What do they care about?
>> What do they value?
>> What have they become?
>> And what differences have I made?
>
> Reflect on these questions. Notice that none of them refers to grades.
>   So, consider the long view. You chose to teach because you believe you can make a difference. You are responsible for those in your care. You should know what you want for them. Regardless of the demands for testing and accountability, you understand in your heart of hearts that your obligation and responsibility to your students is to help them become good people.
>   You articulate what to learn, understand, and be able to do—every class, every day throughout the year. You provide the means for them to assess what they are learning. And you design instruction that reaches out to all learners.

"If you find this way of thinking challenging, I do not blame you," said Mr. Harding. "Perhaps a more deliberate way to plan would be helpful. I discovered late in the twentieth century Grant Wiggins and Jay McTighe's *Understanding by Design*.[1] I recommend that you read their book and check out their website.[2] Let me tell you my perspective":

> Backward design has become an essential tool for classroom teachers. Its principles and practices are comprehensive and accessible, albeit sometimes complex. It hits a "sweet spot." When using it, you not only see the whole but how all of its parts fit. You sense alignment and coherence. You see yourself moving in harmony alongside your budding scholars.
>   Everyone's on the same page. Everyone knows where they're headed. You design effective lessons and enact formative assessment practices that let students know how they are progressing. The hallmark of this approach: They

are with you. They're not in no-man's land. Together you see the end of the tunnel.

Something else happens. Backward-design thinking, at least for me, invokes the spirit. When you become immersed, you're not only engaged but emotionally committed; you experience this often.

Unlike implementing traditional curriculum units, ones handed to you via textbooks, backward design requires engagement. You become involved and want to collaborate with colleagues. And you invite students into the process: informing them where they are headed, how they're assessed, and what they have to do to get there.

Mr. Harding took a breath. "I suggest that you take some time this weekend, Meera and Joyce, and write end-of-the-year reflections. Begin by envisioning your new students leaving your classroom on their last day. Use the questions I listed in my handout. And try to articulate your overall purpose—the purpose of your units and lessons—the big picture. And ponder my favorite question: What is your ultimate backward design?

"Trust that after completing this reflection, you will have a clearer sense of your purpose and be better able to design coherent learning. Having a vision of the whole is essential. It becomes your benchmark. You are in the business of change. Change happens before your eyes. Your lessons change, too, once they come in contact with students. You need to design learning in which you can direct these changes toward worthwhile and productive goals. And successful change, after all, begins at the end. Mrs. Smith and I would be glad to read your reflections."

Meera took a deep breath. This was a lot to take in. No one spoke about backward design in her training. "I sense invoking this process will bring greater focus to my lessons. So many kids are preoccupied with their on-screen lives, so much so that they hardly know they're walking into my class. If I can provide a road map and keep it in front of them, I believe they'll see my classroom as a station where they can reboard the train they were on yesterday. But if there's no connecting pieces, there won't be a track on which to proceed. Every day I'd have to reinvite them to focus—and that would take time! And there would be no coherence."

Joyce liked Meera's metaphor. She had some appreciation for the backward-design mind-set, one she'd briefly heard about. She'd begun to consider its implications but now was convinced that she needed to use it. She wondered if she could make good use of tablets for articulating it, perhaps using Google Drive. Her kids could collaborate in reaching the end in view for a unit. She was looking forward to writing her end-of-the year reflection, as writing has the power to unveil ideas.

Chapter 4

The veterans smiled. Mrs. Smith, who'd been quiet, said, "I'd like to share an idea I learned from Robert Fried in his book *The Passionate Teacher*.[3] Fried wrote about Dan Bisaccio, a New Hampshire teacher now at Brown University, who gave out his biology final exam on the first day of school. Here was a teacher who understands end-of-the-year thinking."

"But how could he possibly do that?" asked Joyce. "If I gave out my final on the first day, my department would freak out. Exams have been given for generations—and some people claim they indicate one's level of intelligence. Not to have exams defies tradition."

"Let me tell you, Joyce and Meera, about Bisaccio's final," said Mrs. Smith. She handed them a copy (see Appendix, "Biology Final Exam," p. 139). "Look closely at the exam: Bisaccio sets up his students to become biologists who seek answers to questions throughout the year, questions that focus on 'the study of life and how organisms relate to their physical environs.' He lists seven, each demanding new evidence every time his students answer. By June they will, in essence, become 'sophisticated biologists.'

"You can see how this relates to backward-design thinking. Dan Bisaccio has a clear vision of what he wants his students to know, understand, and be able to do. He watches his biologists' progress throughout the year. He doesn't focus on completing the curriculum. By the time they walk out the door on the last day, he'll know what they've accomplished—and so will they."

"You know," Joyce said, "if I were to view my students as historians rather than as having to learn history facts, dates, and so forth, I could set up a final like Bisaccio's. I'll have to do some thinking."

Meera chimed in: "I want to take this idea of giving the final on the first day seriously. If I do, my students would see the train we're on—and without my having to prod. In June, we'd arrive at the last stop knowing what we know."

"Here's another approach for framing the big picture," Mrs. Smith said. "Toward the end of my career I borrowed from an article by Bill McKibben[4] to explain my purpose for studying ancient history." She handed out an excerpt.

> Footprints. It's all about footprints.
> The human species emerged on earth some four million years ago.... We live in an ever-expanding world where population has increased fourfold in the past 150 years—from 1.5 billion to nearly six billion! What does all this mean with respect to ancient history? For us, it opens at the time when humans began to distinguish themselves as a species. In the end, it all has to do with footprints—and with the development of consciousness.

"After describing the course beginning with hunter-gathers, the early Far East, Hebrews, Sumerians, Egypt, Greeks, and Romans—what everyone understood as ancient history—I concluded":

> The rise of Western civilization and the coming of the industrial revolution, humans fully implemented these patterns to become lords of the planet. Coca-Cola is everywhere.
>
> As we evolved, we've created something special beyond the creation of civilized cultures. We are the first to be conscious of our consciousness. We can ask, Are we alone? What are we made of? Perhaps the most significant question, best expressed by the great sages, is this: What is our purpose?
>
> Given the exponential growth of the human presence, we live in a world that demands our full attention in order to survive. The ancients provided us with the power to create and savor as well as the power to dominate and destroy. We need to study them to learn how we came to create such large footprints. We need to learn their wisdom, a wisdom that can deepen and enlighten our consciousness and help us succeed on our planet. We are about to embark upon a wonderful adventure together—in class and hopefully on the earth in this special time in which we live.

Meera and Joyce took time to absorb Mrs. Smith's "Footprints." Meera was struck with the image, "Coca-Cola is everywhere." It let young readers instantly realize the world is one—interconnected; people no longer separated; a perfect image—and yet one fraught with challenges. Joyce added that she liked the perspective in the last paragraph, and had she been in the class she would have taken ancient history seriously.

"Besides," Joyce said, "it is hard for adolescents to think beyond their circle. Yet, Mrs. Smith, your effort must have been worth it. I intend to provide a framework for my ever-present, digitally obsessed kids. If I don't try, how will I know whether this approach can work?"

Meera added, "I like that you put in writing where you were headed. I will try that approach, too."

"Thank you, Joyce and Meera," said Mrs. Smith. "By the way, I also sent 'Footprints' home with in-class expectations: 'Pay attention every day, participate in class activities, speak with respect to others, be collaborative, and realize that you make a difference.' My parents signed and returned it."

Mr. Harding spoke up, "I'd like to return for a few minutes to 'what is an ideal doorman?' I applied this concept in visualizing my ideal classroom: the nature of its physical space, quality of personal relationships, treat students as valued guests, focus on accomplishment, emphasize lifelong learning, invoke face-to-face conversation, and create a culture of appreciation. Thinking of the ideal improved the quality of my teaching, and it clearly helped give my classroom its own identity."

"My goodness, another idea!" said Joyce. "Already I have more to think about than I did in graduate school, or at least it sure feels that way!"

"Me too," said Meera. "I think it's because you and I, Joyce, have had a real taste of the classroom, so Mr. Harding and Mrs. Smith's ideas have a context. However, I wish I could have had an internship like doctors have, where I could work alongside either one of you. I know that I would become a better teacher more quickly."

"No doubt," agreed Joyce.

"And Mrs. Smith and I have one more big-picture idea for you to take away," said Mr. Harding. "It has been floating around the Internet where a colleague discovered it. You can find many versions. Let me pass out a copy as I read it":

An expert is speaking to a group of business students, and to drive home a point, he uses an illustration those students will never forget.

As he stands in front of the group of high-powered overachievers, he says, "Okay, time for a quiz." He pulls out a one-gallon, wide-mouthed mason jar and sets it on a table in front of him. Then he produces about a dozen fist-sized rocks and carefully places them, one at a time, into the jar. When the jar is filled to the top and no more rocks fit inside, he asks, "Is this jar full?"

Everyone in the class says, "Yes."

Then he says, "Really?" He reaches under the table and pulls out a bucket of gravel. He dumps some gravel in and shakes the jar causing pieces of gravel to work themselves down into the spaces between the big rocks. Then he asks the group once more, "Is the jar full?"

By this time, the class is onto him. "Probably not," one of them answers.

"Good!" he replies. He reaches under the table and brings out a bucket of sand. He starts dumping the sand in. It falls into all the spaces left between the rocks and the gravel. Once more, he asks the question, "Is this jar full?"

"No!" the class shouts.

Once again, he says, "Good!" Then he grabs a pitcher of water and begins to pour it in until the jar is filled to the brim. Then he looks up at the class and asks, "What is the point of this illustration?"

One eager beaver raises his hand and says, "The point is, no matter how full your schedule is, if you try really hard, you can always fit some more things into it!"

"No," the speaker replies, "that's not the point. The truth this illustration teaches us is this: If you don't put the big rocks in first, you'll never get them in at all."

What are the big rocks in your life? A project you want to accomplish? Time with your loved ones? Your faith? Your education? Your finances? A cause? Teaching or mentoring others? Remember to put these big rocks in first or you'll never get them in at all.

So, when reflecting on this story, ask yourself this question: "What are the big rocks in my life or in my teaching?" Then, put those in your jar first.

With big rocks rattling around in their heads, Meera and Joyce thanked Mrs. Smith and Mr. Harding for a great afternoon. They had much to think about—and a writing assignment for the weekend.

"I may never be the same," said Joyce. "Alas, I will have more direction if I can sort out my planning."

"I agree," said Meera. They waved good-bye to their veteran colleagues knowing they'd meet again—and often.

NOTES

1. Grant Wiggins and Jay McTighe, *Understanding by Design* (Alexandria, VA: Association for Supervision and Curriculum Development, 1998).

2. Authentic Education at authenticeducation.org.

3. Robert L. Fried, *The Passionate Teacher: A Practical Guide* (Boston: Beacon Press, 1995).

4. Bill McKibben, "A Special Moment in History," *The Atlantic*, May 1998.

Chapter 5

Teach Students to Think

Terry Rowe and Ivan Deutsch

I had no intention to appear fair and balanced, no intention to entertain different viewpoints—and had every intention to stimulate critical thinking.

Terry Rowe taught social studies for more than thirty years, mostly to eighth graders. Before he became a teacher, he worked in his father's hardware business but found the work tedious and uninteresting. He entered graduate school to become a teacher. He would earn less money, but he'd be following his heart. An average student in school, he was curious and somewhat precocious. He had an uncanny sense of people around him and was known for his empathy, for seeing others as they see themselves.

He was fearless on the soccer field, often sustaining injury, a reflection of his no-holds-barred attitude. And he liked to taste parts of life he hadn't known. Life as a teacher would be more open to surprise than working with his father. He looked forward to that!

Terry was offered a job at his former high school. After a couple of years, he built a no-nonsense reputation, glaring at misbehaving kids through his wireless glasses from under his unkempt curly hair, raising his eyebrows when hearing something interesting. He was infamous for his "bad" sense of humor—mostly punning—and lively questions, energetic discussions, and creative assignments.

Teaching seemed to come naturally. He worked hard. He listened to his students, not only for their ideas but also to their stories, concerns, and hopes. They knew he was in their camp. In his second year, 1963, his department head, Mort Bronstein, a legend in the school, invited Terry to create a new, dynamic non-Western course to intrigue eighth graders.

Mort and he designed the course to include South Africa, South America, Marxism, and Soviet Communism. Over thirty years, Terry Rowe expanded it to include China and India and cut back the South America and South Africa sections. He liked the opportunity to create his own course, to experiment, modify, tweak, and refine. Passionate about every aspect of his teaching, in his last years near the turn of the century, he incorporated web sources and word processing. Since retirement, he has kept an active interest in his former school.

Ivan Deutsch will be the third person to teach Mr. Rowe's course. Having taught for two years at a traditional school, at his interview he was intrigued with what he'd heard about Mr. Rowe. Not only was he famous for his innovations but also for his compassion. While Ivan would no doubt put his own twist on the course—perhaps adding the Middle East and dropping South Africa—he wanted to tap into Mr. Rowe's thinking.

Ivan left no doubt about his enthusiasm. He had been ebullient since childhood, willing to volunteer to try anything new. In college, he began as a chemistry major but turned to history. Tapping into the past to comprehend the present became his love. And he was eager to become creative with young people, whom he saw as a challenge. They seem so preoccupied with staying connected with their phones. He wondered if he could bring them together in his classroom.

As Ivan was prepping for the opening of school, he saw Mr. Rowe in the office. He asked if they could meet and talk. Mr. Rowe agreed to meet the following Saturday morning at McDonald's.

Mr. Rowe arrived carrying a folder, wearing his familiar Lenin worker's cap, a brown vest, and jeans. He bought a coffee and settled in a booth near the back window. His hair by now was deep gray, his eyes blue, and he had some gray facial hair; his wireless glasses were his trademark. He was looking forward to meeting the young man who would be following his footsteps. Ivan, beyond eager, arrived on time a few minutes later. After buying his coffee, he expressed his thanks to Mr. Rowe for being willing to meet with him and asked if he would share how he came to develop the course.

"Well, interesting you asked, Ivan. Recently I've been reflecting on my life, particularly from my childhood days. I'm more aware of how time plays into who we become. As a child, you would not have expected to see the Terry Rowe sitting here. Let me share a couple of incidents. Growing up in my neighborhood, I tended to be bossy with my friends. In a letter I discovered a few years ago, my camp director had written to my parents." Mr. Rowe reached into his folder:

Terry had difficulty at times restraining his enthusiasm and natural high spirits and at first was inclined to be impatient and critical of other boys with less ability than he has. As the summer advanced he improved markedly, learning to consider the welfare of others as he realized that the right thing was to work for the good of the group rather than just for himself.

"And the following year the director wrote again":

As captain of the Grey Team, Terry took his position over-seriously and was rather more severe than necessary when his teammates did not do their best.

"I've wondered how I would have reacted had I read the letters at that time. I doubt, however, that I would have changed. Let me share another memory with you, Ivan. After playing in a junior high football game, our teams were having hot chocolate. I turned to a boy from the other team and blurted, 'Ha, ha! We won, you lost!' That scene is frozen in my mind: nothing about the game, all about me and winning—and I felt immediate shame. Where did those words come from? Where did the shame come from? That couldn't have been me? Why did I do it? I've asked this question to this day.

"Something must have clicked somewhere along the line. By the time I was in high school, humility found some space in my life; not much, but enough to change direction. I'm not sure why, but I'm glad. If I may, Ivan, pay attention to who you are and how you got to where you are. Knowing yourself will make you a better teacher: You'll be honest, vulnerable, and receptive. By being yourself, you'll project that message onto your kids."

"I appreciate your candidness, Mr. Rowe. You've given me much to think about. As for the course, I'm anticipating teaching kids who've grown up with smartphones, something not familiar to me when I was in school. I'm hope you will give me some doorways that I can pass through to reach them. If I teach the way I was taught—mostly by teachers doing most of the talking—I will not make it, nor will my students."

"You're right, Ivan. Let me begin by sharing the time I first taught Marxism. It was my second year, in the early 1960s during the Cold War. I could not have been more nervous. Mort Bronstein, department head, had convinced me the previous spring to move down to the eighth grade and design a course on South Africa, South America, and Russian and Soviet history and culture. A wide-open door, but a great responsibility. When we came to Karl Marx, I wanted Marx and his philosophy to come alive.

"I knew that Mort would support me. A week before the course, he suggested that I begin with his list of six preconditions of socialism." Mr. Rowe reached into his folder and handed Ivan that list:

1. There must be an obvious and deep-rooted inequality between economic classes—and little hope that this inequality can be easily, or will be shortly, straightened out.
2. There must be a feeling that this inequality is an injustice—that this injustice should and can be corrected.
3. There must be a feeling that all persons, of whatever circumstances and conditions, deserve equitable treatment, not equal treatment, that deserving people should receive a fair share of the world's worldly goods.
4. There must be a basic belief that many, or most, of the people of the world are basically good and therefore want to cooperate for the good of all.
5. There must be a belief that these good people should control the economy—and necessarily the entire society.
6. The organizers of the socialist impulse must be good intellectuals.

Ivan took time to read them. He was impressed with their broad scope and coverage of fundamental principles. Mr. Rowe then told the story of the first time he put them in front of his eighth graders:

"I set a different tone. My first two units, South Africa and South America, had been somewhat conventional: paperbacks, ditto sheets, films, lecture-discussions, and guest speakers. I concluded with a South American festival held in my classroom complete with two hay stalls, a live goat, and a piñata.

"However, before the first class on Marx, Ivan, I pulled down the shades, placed black paper on the clear glass of my door, turned off half the lights, and switched on the overhead—my classroom an inner sanctum. Projecting on the overhead, I put, 'Today we'll discuss the preconditions of socialism.' My unsuspecting eighth graders entered hesitantly, their thirteen-year-old faces scanning the room and murmuring as they found their desks: 'Why has Mr. Rowe pulled down the shades?' 'Why does the room feel so dark?' 'Is he about to do something bad?'

"For the next two days, I processed the six preconditions. Imagine, Ivan, imagine listening in on our conversations. For the first precondition, I heard such responses as, 'There *is* a natural inequality between classes'; 'inequality *is* what makes America work'; 'having more education *entitles* people to more income.' In response to the second: 'Inequality is not an injustice, it's the way the world is.' And to the fourth: 'How can everyone be basically good when the world is in turmoil with Hitler, Mussolini, and others who have hurt the world'; 'but if the world were evil, we would not be here, as it takes good people to keep the world going.'

"And for the sixth, Ivan, I appealed to their egos: 'Here, class, is where you come in. I'm offering you the opportunity to become 'good intellectuals.' You will be on the ground floor ready for the revolution and join what Marx calls, 'the vanguard.' Your intimacy with socialist principles will enable you to explain them to others, as I'm explaining them to you.'"

Looking back, Mr. Rowe confessed to Ivan that when he was teaching these preconditions, he was only vaguely familiar with them. "But the conversations were not *about something*, not about what we read about, talked about, nor was it about taking quizzes and finally having a test. No, these conversations put us *inside socialist thinking*, inside the socialist mind-set. I didn't know whether I could pull off such a controversial topic. And it was at the height of the Cold War! Thank goodness, Mort Bronstein stayed close.

"Inculcating the preconditions was a new doorway. We became immersed. I *was* Karl Marx, pontificating from my heart that socialism, then communism, would triumph over capitalism. I never let up as we transitioned into Soviet history. I hope you, Ivan, will discover the power of immersion and incorporate it into what you're teaching and feel its rewards."

Ivan took a deep breath. His teacher preparation had been about designing lessons, taking methods courses, and reading educational philosophy—all useful—but nothing like Mr. Rowe's portrayal. Ivan was well-tuned to technology: the Internet to access the world; YouTube as a bottomless source of video; and the iPad for in-class writing, research, and collaboration—screen time together. Yet he was convinced that if he were to make history come alive, he would have to do it face to face, through the art of discussion. His students would have to put their phones away—far away.

"You know," Mr. Rowe, "I'm going to put Mr. Bronstein's six preconditions on my SMART board. I want to see how my kids respond, how curious they are about each precondition. I wonder what kind of discussions will emerge? I will sit back, listen, and wait for comments if I must. If I were to offer opinions, especially early on, I could block some students from sharing theirs."

Mr. Rowe liked this plan—especially Ivan's willingness to step back. He asked Ivan to let him know how it worked. He then continued sharing his early experience with Marx. He recounted how he conveyed Marx's concept of dialectical materialism, the inexorable law of history as progress from prehistory to feudalism, to capitalism, and finally to communism.

"Marx saw history as progress, Ivan, the result of conflicts in which the opposition (antithesis) confronts those in power (thesis), the result a new level of society (synthesis). From American history: the colonists (antithesis) struggled against England's King George III (thesis) to form a new American democracy (synthesis)." Mr. Rowe handed Ivan diagrams that he'd drawn for his students.

Ivan was fascinated. So many fancy terms for eighth graders! But to have taught Marx with no inhibitions in the time of the Cold War; he didn't think he could have done it. However, he would have been comfortable explaining

Marx's structure of capitalist society to his students: the grande bourgeoisie (.01 percent), the petite bourgeoisie (10–20 percent), and the proletariat (80–90 percent). Then there were the five laws of capitalism: law of surplus value, labor theory of value, law of accumulation, law of concentration, and the law of increasing misery. I wonder how my kids would see this framework in today's United States. What kind of conversations would we have?

"My biggest challenge," Mr. Rowe went on, "came after introducing the Marxian concepts of capitalist exploitation and oppression. I told them that they—and I—as members of the petite bourgeoisie class, were oppressors. But how could I, a good person, think of myself as an oppressor and tell my students that they'll become oppressors? But the more I talked about it, the easier it became. Let me show you, Ivan, a composite of the conversations I had around capitalist oppression." He pulled out another paper from his folder (see Appendix, "Examples of Capitalist Oppression," p. 144). "Let's go over a couple of examples":

> The police: You know what they do? First and foremost, they protect property. Who owns property in a capitalist society? The grande bourgeoisie! Everything they do goes back to protecting property!
>
> And the sanctity of the family! How marvelous it is to be a mother! The family is a unit to keep people happy—an artificial one at that. The family is our opiate, a device to make us forget our troubles, the miseries outside. A place of order and tranquility.

"You should have seen the look on their faces, Ivan. I zipped through all of them to instill a sense of awe. I had no intention to appear fair and balanced, no intention to entertain different viewpoints—and had every intention to stimulate critical thinking. Over four periods a day, I shared Marxian ideology. Each time I deepened my understanding, becoming a knowledgeable Marxist. I felt fortunate! And I was learning as much as they.

"I concluded with Marx by softening my tone," Mr. Rowe said leaning back in his chair. "Socialism, after all, Ivan, is a descriptive term, not a judgment; the same is true for capitalism. Each has its role to play in history. Capitalism has suffered from depressions and wars, as seen in the Great Depression and two world wars. Social Security, so important to many people, can be understood as a device created by the grande bourgeoisie to stave off rebellion, to keep people happy; otherwise, they might revolt. And socialism has its own vulnerabilities.

"One class, when I was sharing Marx's infamous 'Religion is the opiate of the people' quote, a girl burst into tears: 'That's not true, Mr. Rowe. My church is not like that! I love my church!' As badly as I was feeling for her, much like a father who has overstepped his parenting, my efforts to instill the 'Gospel According to Marx' was having its hoped-for effect. I paused, lowered my voice, and quietly said, 'Well, Mia, see what you think when you read what Marx wrote in the *Communist Manifesto*.'

"The *Communist Manifesto* is short, concise, and proved surprisingly accessible—for Marx at least. After lively conversations over several days of absorbing Marx's own words, Ivan, we came to the end of Marx's diatribe." Mr. Rowe took out another paper from his folder:

> A good Marxist knows well these words: "What the bourgeoisie therefore produces, above all, are its own gravediggers. Its fall and the victory of the proletariat are equally inevitable. . . . In place of the old bourgeois society, with its classes and class antagonisms, we shall have an association, in which the free development of each is the condition for the free development of all."
>
> And finally: "Let the ruling classes tremble at a Communistic revolution. The proletarians have nothing to lose but their chains. They have a world to win. Working men of all countries, unite!"

"No one questioned my approach, Ivan: that I pulled down the shades and papered the window on my door, acted as a promoter of socialism and communism—and had the audacity to assign the *Communist Manifesto*. No parents complained. No letters appeared in the local papers. And the communist threat loomed large! Perhaps Mort Bronstein protected me. I liked to think that my parents trusted what I was doing.

"I can imagine the challenge of taking this approach today. While we're no longer in the Cold War, we live in a time of intense political dialogue where professing 'the other side' finds no common ground. I could see parents barraging the school were I to avow what would be perceived as 'anti-American.' Yet, I think it's worth immersing students inside content. It's worth taking on the polarization of our culture. This may be a delicate task for you, Ivan, but well worth pursuing."

After Mr. Rowe departed, Ivan took a deep breath. He did not expect to have learned so much from one session. He'd been with a man who spoke from a deep place. His words were deliberate, confident in its message, and attentive to his audience. He must have been a presence in his classroom. "I would like to have been there," Ivan said to himself.

He wondered how he could make his course have a Mr. Rowe impact. In the fifty years since Mr. Rowe taught Marx, Ivan would have access to unlimited sources on the Internet; a SMART board to bring these sources into the classroom—no need to copy, paste, and print out; and he could invoke lessons using his school's iPad class sets. He'd find free books, YouTube videos, and other resources. And he would relegate all smartphones—turned off—into cubbies and engage his kids' curiosity by encouraging conversation, lots of conversation.

Mr. Rowe was delighted; his new protégé was such an eager listener. They agreed to meet in a couple of Fridays after school when he would share his early years expounding on Soviet Communism in the Soviet Union—this time at the Xentano Café not far from the school.

Chapter 6

Explore the Other Side

Terry Rowe and Ivan Deutsch

Students ignite! You have nothing to lose but your oppression. You have the Grande Bourgeoisie to burn.

Ivan Deutsch and Mr. Rowe arrived at the Xentano Café at the same time. Finding a table in the back corner, they sat down with their coffee—and Mr. Rowe, a donut. Ivan thanked him for the intriguing conversation on Marx. He was already thinking about how he could use an immersion approach in exploring the U.S.–Russian relationship.

Before moving on to talk about teaching the Soviet Union, Ivan shared the day he put the six preconditions of socialism on his SMART board.

"My students and I had quite the conversations. The first one on 'deep-rooted inequality between economic classes' hit a nerve. I sense that a lot of young people are concerned about this issue. They are fair-minded lot, Mr. Rowe. Frankly, I was surprised.

"For the second, people receiving 'a fair share of the world's goods' got almost as much attention. Again, it showed their concern for fairness. Almost to a person, they faulted movements that divide people, ones that put some in unfair advantageous positions. I was impressed with their willingness to express their ideas—and listen to others. I think I've made some progress having an engaging classroom. Thanks for sharing the preconditions, Mr. Rowe."

For the next hour and a half, Mr. Rowe recounted his approach to the Soviet Union at the height of the Cold War. He began by telling Ivan that he found a paperback text that took a historical approach; it allowed him to share his love of Russian history before digging into Soviet times.[1] Once his students had a clear picture of Russian geography and early history, he put the book aside. He handed out a one-page, five-paragraph "brief history" that he received from the Soviet Embassy in Washington. "Here, to the best of my memory, Ivan, is how I introduced it." Mr. Rowe cleared his throat:

> Good afternoon, class. You have before you a one-page, five-paragraph summary of Russian and Soviet history. You are to act as detectives—like Sherlock Holmes or Perry Mason [a popular TV detective at the time]—and figure out who wrote this, why did they write it, and who was it for? We will take all the time we need to find the answers.

"When I first read the brief history, I was tempted to process it paragraph by paragraph; I'd be sure that everyone would get it. After all, that was a technique most of my teachers used. They believed it was the best way to assure everyone understood what was in front of them.

"You may not believe it, but these kids spent two periods analyzing the five paragraphs among themselves—all four of my classes! They questioned whether it was factual, interpretive, or propaganda. In the end they agreed it was a Soviet publication designed to persuade readers about the virtues of the U.S.S.R. They had the most difficulty, however, with the final paragraph. Take a look":

> The main principles of the Soviet Union's foreign policy are: the peaceful coexistence of states with different social systems, non-interference in the internal affairs of other states, the strengthening and expansion of economic and cultural ties between nations, the struggle for general disarmament, the averting of wars and the strengthening of world peace.

"I remember being so excited about the process that I burst out with gratitude. Something about giving them that time—a luxury you may not have—and being patient brought great satisfaction. I was discovering how to be a leader *and* a participant. Had we stayed in the textbook, who knows, I might still be standing at the front of the room, the one in charge, the one responsible for being sure that they 'got it.' I hope, Ivan, you will find ways to release your students to be detectives—and stand back to watch and listen.

"Another document came from a Soviet English-language school textbook that parodied life in America."[2] Mr. Rowe handed Ivan a copy.

> Three dirt-poor children, Willie, Jack, and Mary, live in a tumbledown house in an impoverished coal-mining town and never get enough to eat. When Willie tells his teacher that Mary could not come to school because it was so cold and she had no winter coat, the teacher retorts:
>
> "Well, why doesn't your mother buy one?"
>
> "My mother has no money," Willie says. "Dad gets very little pay. We even haven't enough to eat."

"Well," says the teacher, "It's because your father is lazy. If he worked harder, he would get money for his work."

"No, Miss Smith, it is because the boss is greedy. My dad works very, very hard but it doesn't do him any good."

"Don't you dare talk back to me, Willie," cries the teacher angrily. "If you do, you will be left back."

"No one had any concept of the life of such poor people," said Mr. Rowe. "But what became disturbing was the teacher's attitude—an anathema to them. You should have been there!"

"Come on, Mr. Rowe, do you believe this stuff? No way would anyone believe this!"
"Why would the teacher blame the father?"
"How can she call the father lazy when he works very hard?"
"Leaving a kid back because he talks back to her, no way!"

"My kids figured out this anecdote served as an example of how Soviet authorities propagandized the shortcomings of capitalism. There could be no other explanation. Let me show you another document, which also proved provocative." He handed him a list of twenty duties Soviet schoolchildren were expected to follow (see Appendix, "Duties of Soviet Schoolchildren," p. 140).

Ivan took a few minutes to read the duties. "You must have had some interesting discussions!"
"Let's examine a few of them," said Mr. Rowe:

It is the duty of every schoolchild . . .

3. To obey without question the orders of the school director and teachers.
8. To sit erect during the lesson period, not leaning on the elbows or slouching in the seat . . . not talking or engaging in mischief.
10. To rise and stand erect while reciting; to sit down only on permission of the teacher; to raise the hand when desiring to answer or ask a question.
12. To be respectful of the school director and the teachers, to greet them on the street with a polite bow, boys removing their hats.

Ivan smiled. "I'd like to use this list without providing background information. I'll ask my students: 'Imagine you were in this school. How would you like to comply to these duties?' 'Which ones would you be willing to follow?' 'Which ones are offensive?' And most important, I'd ask the big question: 'What are the cultural values of this society?' I hope to see lots of discussion, which will provide for a good writing assignment."

Mr. Rowe smiled. He like that his protégé was showing initiative. While it had been more than fifty years since Mr. Rowe had introduced these duties, he recalled almost verbatim some comments. He shared them with Ivan:

- N° 3: One girl said that she did not agree with obeying *without* question the director and teachers; instead they should obey but question with respect.
- N° 8: It appeared as most un-American. Not to be able to lean on your elbows or slouch in your seat? "Gimme a break, Mr. Rowe! What happens to the student who does?" And, "It's okay not to engage in mischief, but to have to sit erect all the time? No way!"
- N° 10: Raising hands, standing to recite, and sitting with teacher's permission: "Raising hands is okay, Mr. Rowe, but to stand erect when speaking makes no sense. And having to stand would really slow down conversations. Weren't those kids allowed to talk with one another?"
- N° 12: On bowing to greet teachers in the street; boys removing their hats: "Not a chance, Mr. Rowe. We would never do that. Not even to you!"

"By the time we finished discussing this list, Ivan, some of my students began to express empathy for Soviet children trapped inside such a formal system. They seemed relieved that they did not have to act as little puppets under a strict regimen. They didn't have to stand when reciting and sit down with the teacher's permission. Then came the day I set up a simulated Soviet classroom."

Ivan and Mr. Rowe ordered another cup of coffee. Already, Ivan's mind was spinning with more ideas. He was beginning to see how he could adapt these materials. He liked Mr. Rowe's use of primary sources that encouraged seeking meaning. Despite having targets to meet for tests, Ivan was beginning to understand that if he stressed critical thinking it would prepare his kids for any test.

With a twinkle in his eye, Mr. Rowe recounted his Soviet classroom relying on his memory and some black-and-white photos that he brought:

> In preparation for that day, my students put a Soviet flag in place of the American flag at the left of the blackboard and stretched above it a painted mural in black-lined watercolor depicting Cossacks. At the back of the room was a graphic of our Soviet school flag, Malomorinsk, with a large red M in the center surrounded by five red Soviet stars.
>
> Above it a sign that read, "He who does not work does not eat," and below a diorama portraying Nikita Khrushchev in a massive, oversized arctic fur coat. Left of the red M, "Songs for the Young Pioneer to Learn." To the right, a compilation of "Student Honors" with hammers, sickles, and ribbons bordering

images of exemplary work. Above, "Courage, Faithfulness, and Love" in large black lettering portraying the class motto.

On the day, Ivan, you would have observed students filing into the room in white shirts and white blouses, dark blue pants and dark blue skirts, each wearing a red Pioneer scarf. These "Soviets" sat in pairs at abutted desks, each prepared to raise his right hand to answer a question while keeping his elbow on the desk, to stand when answering, and sit down only when "Comrade Teacher" granted permission.

"The day could not have been smoother." Mr. Rowe then described the class publication, which emulated Lenin's infamous newspaper, *Iskra* "Volume LXIV, Number One." On its red cover, "All the News That's Red We Print" appeared above a hand-drawn image of a hammer and sickle. The paper's board included editors, publication, layout, and art staff, thirty-one in all with self-created Russian names. In unsigned bylines, reporters were meticulous recounting the day's events and ancillary activities. Mr. Rowe handed Ivan a copy of *Iskra*. He pointed to a sample of the writing:

> Noted Soviet physicist, G. Millerinsky, appeared in a long white science coat and tie, wore glasses, and had closely cropped hair. He showed how the Soviet Union has advanced in scientific matters far beyond the United States and gave a logical, scientific explanation of the natural wonders which naive capitalists attribute to God.
>
> Professor Nutterinsky explained algebra so simply that it presented a strong contrast to the complicated science but could be understood by all.
>
> Popular English teacher, M. MacMillanofsky, with assistance from M. Richmondoff, proved to be able and strict and discouraged any lax habits in carrying out lessons and insisted upon perfect answers at all times. The class tried adjectives after studying transitive and intransitive verbs.

Ivan noticed the quality, attention to detail, restraint of judgment, and a feel for the Soviets. He wondered, too, if his students would be able to write as well.

"Read all of *Iskra*, Ivan, and let me know your impressions. Meanwhile, check this part on page two":

> Mid-morning after several lectures, physical education instructors W. Gloveross and A. Wrightsonofsky led students to the front of the school facing Main Street to participate in Soviet-style exercises. As they marched two-by-two, they recited the "Enthusiasm March," composed by one of their schoolmates:
>
>> We have no fear
>> We recognize no barriers.

Chapter 6

> O'er land and sea
> Through cloud and ice we'll fly.
> Our hearts burn with the flame
> That fills our country's flag.
> We'll bear it on
> Forever forward and high.

"And, Ivan, you will find detailed reports on the rest of the day. Let's take a look at an excerpt on page four":

> After a half-hour of exercises in the front of the school they marched two-by-two back to the classroom. Professor D. Fogginsky, who'd put a series of key questions on the board, lectured on Abraham Lincoln, accompanied by a poem about the president by an American author—unnamed—who denounced Lincoln's policies.
>
> Once the professor completed his lesson, honor students presented research reports from the Marxist perspective on "The Political Situation in the U.S.A.," "Housing Conditions in the U.S.A.," and "Economics of the U.S.A." At the end of the day, the class turned toward the flag at the back of the room. "Hail Khrushchev" was repeated several times, and class was dismissed.

Mr. Rowe explained that he also created a "Meet the Communists" panel. He invited five of his most eager students each to research a Marxist-socialist revolutionary and portray him in front of their classmates. Reaching into his folder, Mr. Rowe handed *Iskra*'s description of each revolutionary for the panel. "This excerpt is rather long, Ivan, but gives you a good idea of the thoroughness of their work":

> Helen Schultzsky, tall, somewhat shy, and an excellent reader, tied her long hair below her neck to impersonate Karl Marx. Adam Laddovsky, among the most active in class, wore a coat and tie with mustache, goatee, and continental cap to become Vladimir Ilyich Ulyanov (Lenin).
>
> Sumner Rollinoftsky, gregarious, bright, and whimsical, put on a Russian military jacket and flaunted the mustached Joseph Stalin. Ellen Borisonoft, demur but forceful, in glasses, goatee, mustache, dark coat and pants, and continental-styled necktie, took on the role of the unpopular Leon Trotsky. And John Stebbinsky, a future lawyer in the making, attired in a light blue suit with silk tie and a pillow stuffed under his shirt, became the colorful Nikita Khrushchev.
>
> For each session, the panel members sat in front of a class and stated their role in Soviet history. The room was attentive, the questions sharp, especially from *Iskra*'s journalists:
>
> *Iskra*: Karl Marx, why didn't you demonstrate that socialism is better than capitalism?

Marx: A genius has so many ideas and plans that he wanted to work on, that he could do only what he could. . . . I died before I got around to it and had to leave it for someone else to finish.

Iskra: Mr. Stalin, why did you purge so many of your people?

Stalin: You have a bourgeois interpretation of this very private and personally Soviet occurrence. All societies must dispose of their deceased elements. We have chosen our method.

Iskra: Mr. Trotsky, why did you issue Decree #903, which allowed an increasing number of commanders to arrest as hostage all members of the family?

Trotsky: If one person in the family deserts, he has influence on the rest of the family, so the whole family should be arrested.

Iskra: Vladimir Ilyich Lenin, why did you assign a wrecking crew to expropriate the expropriators?

Lenin: We had masses of proletarians working behind us, therefore we had the power to expropriate the expropriators.

Iskra: Mr. Khrushchev, why does the Soviet Union practice with nuclear weapons but always says it does not want war with the U.S.?

Khrushchev: These tests are held only for defensive purposes, because the U.S. is also testing. But I know that the U.S. does not want to start a nuclear war either.

"Mr. Rowe," Ivan said, leaning forward in his chair, "I'm impressed with the intimate knowledge your 'revolutionaries' expressed, and the quality of the reporters' questions. How did you decide who should be on the panel? How did you choose the reporters? Where did your students find research materials? How much time did you allow for them to prepare?"

"Some from my top section volunteered and pretty much prepared on their own," Mr. Rowe said with a smile. "I trusted them, Ivan. I had to allow them time if they were to have any chance to succeed. The panelists and *Iskra* reporters, who also volunteered, immersed themselves, each one committed to excellence and eager to learn on their own—a process they came to love. I saw them as Olympians."

Ivan wondered if he could allow such freedom with his kids—and if his department would tolerate it.

Mr. Rowe was on a roll, becoming animated as he rekindled his memory of those days. "Do you mind if I indulge in one more concept, one that I discovered the first year I taught this unit? Instead of giving regular tests, I devised Communist-centered exams. I wanted to stay inside the aura I was creating; in essence, not to have my students step away and 'look in' on what we had been doing. Here's one example":

Chapter 6

> Order of the Young Pioneers
> Examination #1 by order of Comrade Rowe
> for Eighth Grade Intelligence Division
> on this day of November 24
> in the year of the frontier, 1964

You will become some of the first Americans to join the wave of the future. Your contribution will prove to be a catalyst in developing the inevitability of man's destiny. Your decision to join this movement will push forward the already operating inexorable laws of history.

Students ignite! You have nothing to lose but your oppression! You have the Grande Bourgeoisie to burn!

A good capitalist like a good socialist must be certain to learn as much as he can as well as he can. Even if you do not favor the socialist view, is it not logical that you must learn and understand the socialist view?

We thank you for your cooperation. Keep your spirits up, your heads high, and be aware of the world around you.

> Yours in Communism,
> Comrade Rowe

Ivan read it slowly. "Had I been in your classroom, I might have been perplexed. How did they react to these tests? Did they believe they would 'become some of the first Americans to join the wave of the future'?"

"I don't think I ever asked them, Ivan. However, by now they'd become used to me, to my shenanigans, if you will. They treated the tests seriously, and I did not make them difficult.

"And here are two more items from *Iskra* to whet your appetite. The first an excerpt the editorial board drafted with help from me; the second one I wrote":

THE TIME HAS COME
   Too long have we waited for this glorifying moment, when the minds of the people shall awaken to the stirring thought of rebellion against the Grande Bourgeoisie.... Now is the time for you, the oppressed victims of the American Grande Bourgeoisie, to arise and crush the Capitalists with the omnipotent implements of Communism: atheism and materialism.... Citizens of America, IGNITE, and fight for your rights as a Communist!
   WHY?
   Iskra is here, because the American student has the right to project himself into the pulse of another nation. *Iskra* is the expression of this right. We have "been" Lenin, Stalin, Marx, and Khrushchev; we have "interviewed" these notables. We have "lived" in a Soviet classroom; we have "felt" the pressures of being dogmatically disciplined.
   Iskra is a privilege. We cherish it.

Mr. Rowe looked at his watch and suggested they've covered enough. Ivan agreed but wanted to have more conversations. He would take a close look at Mr. Rowe's materials: How to have his students live inside other cultures—to know the "other side"—and come to understand it; how to make seeking meaning his focus, not simply obtaining knowledge, which tests seem to mandate. These principles would become his mantra. It would mean more work but would be well worth it.

For his Russian unit, Ivan would begin with Putin but take his kids back to Soviet times via Mr. Rowe's pathways, perhaps helping to clarify how and why Putin had become a dictator. He would use the *Iskra* newspaper concept but transform it into a digital website or blog, a more familiar form. He would look for ideas in RT America, the Russian TV channel based in Washington, DC, for America. The apple didn't fall far from the tree; from the tsars to Stalin, and now to Putin, and Ivan hoped his apples wouldn't be far from Mr. Rowe's tree.

Before they left the café, Mr. Rowe said, "Whenever I tell people about my having inculcated Marxism and Soviet Communism during the 1960s, they raise their eyebrows: 'Why did you dare to try to make your students believe Marxist socialism?' 'Why did you attempt to have them empathize with Soviet Communism?' 'It's one thing to role play a Soviet classroom, but don't you think publishing a Communist newspaper is going way too far?' Now more than fifty years later, Ivan, I would have done it all again. No hesitation."

And as far as Mr. Rowe knew, none of his former students had become Marxist revolutionaries, but they have become critical thinkers. Many had told him, "Mr. Rowe, you taught me how to think."

"You can't do better than that, Mr. Rowe," Ivan said with a smile.

NOTES

1. Alfred J. Rieber and Robert C. Nelson, *A Study of the USSR and Communism: An Historical Approach* (Chicago: Scott Foresman, 1962).

2. Leften Stavrianos, et al., *Readings in World History* (Boston: Allyn and Bacon, 1966), 390–91.

Chapter 7

Using Grading to Improve Learning

George Persons and Harold Coughlin

> *As of today, each of you has an A for the year. That's it. An A for the year.*

Harold Coughlin had been teaching for five years. He was tempted to leave the profession a year earlier but decided against it. He was frustrated trying to engage his students, to have them commit to reading and writing. Not that he was a dinosaur in this digital age, but he believed they should be able to read thoughtfully, exercise curiosity, discuss among themselves, and write to reveal their thinking and arguments.

Instead, he saw them relying on texting, Snapchat, and Twitter: short bursts of information, not thoughts, jumping one to another. Between all of this, he thought, the average student must check his or her phone well over 150 times a day. And their attention spans in class were limited. Sometimes he thought that Barbara Ehrenreich was right, that "smartphone screens seemed to have swallowed the world."[1] But when Harold felt that he might have a slim chance of winning his kids over, he decided to stay.

He was one of the young cadre in his school who some on the faculty called the hope of the future. These young teachers were bringing an awareness of the digital impact on kids but were struggling. Harold felt even farther out of the loop, as he did not spend his social time on his phone as much as some of his friends; certainly nowhere near as much as his students.

As a ninth-grade social studies/language arts teacher, he'd adapted to his school's curricula. He recognized that some of it might appear old fashioned, but he did his best to enliven his presentations and assignments. The more he practiced, the closer he seemed to get. His *Grapes of Wrath* unit had become popular, as had his nonfiction choices: Malcolm Gladwell's *The Tipping Point* and Martin Luther King Jr.'s *I Have a Dream/Letter from Birmingham*

Jail. As for assessments, he tended to give spot quizzes and tests, sometimes with short-answer questions, fill-in-the-blank, true-false, and an essay or two.

Harold saw his tests as hit or miss. Some students did well, most did average, and several failed. In his first year, he noticed those who failed after a couple of tests tended to give up. "Why try to do well when I already have two F's?" they told him. Harold decided to implement his own grading scale, one he'd heard about at a workshop. Instead of a scale from 0 to 100, he set up one that was 0 to 5. A student with a failed grade needed only to do one point better to pass rather than make up sixty points. It might be psychological, Harold thought, but he had seen it work.

Because of his concern about grading, Harold decided to seek the wisdom of George Persons, a veteran close to retirement. Mr. Persons, who recently came to the high school science department, was well-known for his innovative ways to teach, finding approaches to break through the apathy of his screen-based students. Harold, who'd briefly met Mr. Persons, left him a note in his mailbox to ask if they could meet after school. Mr. Persons agreed to meet Friday afternoon in the lounge at the town library, a well-known meeting place.

Harold heard that Mr. Persons stayed clear of digital devices as much as possible; he had a basket in which his students had to put their turned-off phones. Harold didn't know if Mr. Persons used a computer or had a smartphone, but he knew he was a creative teacher and cared about his students.

Harold wasn't surprised to find Mr. Persons engrossed in a book in a lounge chair near the back corner of the room, his gold-rimmed glasses down his nose, one hand holding the book, the other under his chin. He looked at peace, probably doing what he loved. Harold imagined him as a young teacher in front of his students with the same look of ease. When he stood and introduced himself, Harold heard his smooth, firm, assured tone. He imagined that he would have liked to have been in Mr. Persons's classroom.

After exchanging pleasantries, Harold asked, "Would you be willing to talk about grading? Someone told me that you have developed your own approaches. Dealing with grades has been frustrating; they interrupt the flow of relationships and continuity of my teaching. I wish that I did not have to grade."

Mr. Persons smiled; he understood Harold's conundrum. "In my first two years in the high school, I was determined to have students work hard. I made them earn their A's and B's. As a result, I developed a reputation, becoming nicknamed, 'Mr. C,' which was the likely grade in my classes. The guidance office was not pleased. When I moved down to the junior high, I relaxed my attitude and put less emphasis on grades. Then in my third year, Harold, take a listen to this: Imagine yourself in my class on the first day of school as I announced . . ." Mr. Persons stood up as if he was before his class:

> Welcome to our first day. I've been looking forward to being with you, as other teachers have told me good things. No doubt, you've heard stories about me; I hope mostly positive. Because you are 8-1's, the top section (we had tracking in those days), I've decided to change my grading policy with you. I'm doing this because I've noticed that top-section students seem to put grades first and learning second. So, here's my proposal. As of today, each of you has an A for the year. That's it. An A for the year. You'll now be free to focus on learning and not worry about your grade. You are the top eighth-grade section, after all, and have been since fourth grade. So, whatever you do or don't do [Mr. Persons raised his voice for emphasis], I will put an A on your report card for each marking period and your final grade.

"At first, no one said anything, Harold. I can still hear some of the questions."

> "What if I don't do my homework?"
> "You will still get an A."
> "What if I flunk my tests, Mr. Persons?"
> "You'll get your A."
> "OK, Mr. Persons, what if I fail to do a long assignment like writing a paper?"
> "No problem, Eric" (I can't forget him; this redhead always challenged me),
>   "you'll still get your A. I am serious, I want you to forget about grades and focus on what we'll be learning. This class will be about learning first and always."

Noticing Harold's look of surprise, Mr. Persons said that he did this only once. And he'd done it without asking or telling anyone—not the guidance office, not his department head. "It was a whim, Harold," Mr. Persons said, "plain and simple. Sometimes whims turn out well, other times not so; probably not the best way to act in a school. But at the time I felt I could be me in my classroom, to do what I believed was best for everyone. Signing a contract did not restrict me from being the person I was. I saw myself as a maverick.

"In this instance, I got away with it. Students from other classes complained, as did a few colleagues. Some in the class briefly chose not to do their homework, but in class they wrestled with ideas, engaged in lively arguments, and—most interesting—took quizzes, tests, and paper assignments seriously. Good teaching, I discovered, Harold, is a more powerful motivator than the threat of grades. And absent this threat brought us closer together. They knew I was there for them."

"Why did you give A's for the year only once?"

"A very good question. Perhaps it was pressure from others. On second thought, I may have felt it unfair to other students, but no one complained.

If you're intrigued with this notion, I suggest you read 'Giving an A,' in the Zanders' *The Art of Possibility*.[2] Their approach is more effective than my whim from more than forty-five years ago.

"Benjamin Zander, a music professor, was concerned about his conservatory students, who insisted that they play perfectly for him every time he came to see them. He became frustrated with their dog-and-pony shows in order to get their A. Zander wanted to break down this grade barrier and become free to teach.

"He came upon a genius of an idea. He asked them to write a letter to him in the past tense, dated at the end of the term, to explain how they earned their A. Once they passed in their letter, they no longer needed to worry. They could practice in front of him for real—and he could offer feedback. And, Harold—I particularly liked this—if he ever saw one of his musicians not acting as an A student, he reminded her of her commitment."[3]

Harold liked this idea. "I might invite my students to write a letter at the beginning of a month, like Mr. Zander, dated at the end, in which they state the grade they want and how they'll earn it. I think it would help them take ownership in their work, but it would be better if they set their target—A, B, or C, which would be more realistic."

Mr. Persons liked Harold's thinking. He agreed a letter would encourage students to take their role in the classroom more seriously. Instead of relying on what grade the teacher would give, they would have a stake in the process, a step closer to committing to their education.

"Years ago, Harold, I worked in another grading paradigm in the fifth grade at a nearby elementary school—a special hiatus in my career. We did not have to give grades—for quizzes and tests, for each term, or for the year. Instead, we built portfolios of each child's work: all their writing—draft and final copies—art, projects, journals, and our comments; we put 3D work on a shelf.

"Parents would come with their child and review the portfolio. It was the work that spoke, better than a letter grade and comment. We also sent periodic newsletters to parents telling them what we were doing, our expectations, and upcoming units of study. We asked for feedback and invited them to come to observe. However, we did not have many takers. Parents were busy and a school is not easy to walk into.

"Other schools have used portfolios. In some, high schoolers defend their work in public in order to pass to the next level. I once saw students present portfolios to a panel of community members, who weighed in on their success or need for improvement. It was quite an experience, and the students knew their stuff! I never tried that, Harold, but I liked the process.

"And finally, I like Jon Saphier's concept of 'A, B, and not yet,' where B is the standard, A above and beyond.[4] If a school were to adopt this system, it would denote that everyone could learn—and that teachers would do all they could to get them there including tutoring after school, evenings, and on some weekends. I've advocated for this idea, as I abhor the A, B, C, D, F system, which sorts more than educates. However, only a few colleagues have been willing to entertain this idea. Old ways are hard to let go, very hard.

"As you can see I've considered a range of ideas about grading. Perhaps you will find a better one. And may I tell you one more approach—more indirect—that I discovered in middle school and used nearly every year. Imagine you're in my class." Again, Mr. Persons stood.

> "You are free in this class to work as hard as you choose. But whatever study habits you develop, they will travel with you into high school where a transcript follows your every move. This is your last, great dress rehearsal, the time to try your best and see how well you can do. Of course, Harold, some students challenged me.
>
> "Mr. Persons, what if I work hard but don't do well?"
>
> "All I can say, the more you try the better chance you'll become a better student. Don't give up!"
>
> "If I choose not to work hard this year, Mr. Persons, can I pick up next year when, as you say, it counts?"
>
> "Yes, you can make that choice. What I am offering, however, is to encourage you to develop good study habits *now*—and an attitude to want to do your best. After all, you become what you practice. It's really up to you. You can choose to want to learn, to develop knowledge and skills, to ask questions, to challenge one another and me, to state your opinions, to become critical thinkers, to seek the truth. Or you can just sit back and get by."

"Wow! Your approach is another way for students to take more responsibility for their education, and it reinforces the notion that invitations to learn are more powerful than threats. They see you on their side rather than acting as an authority figure."

"You're right. I wish I understood this premise earlier in my career. Yet I never tilted toward the authority side of teaching. However, I did learn about the extreme effects of authoritarianism from my friend, Jon Boylen, who taught in a Soviet school in Leningrad in the late 1980s. He wrote to me":

> The pressure from Moscow central authorities on all schools put students and teachers in peril. In daily lessons, during recitations pupils from the earliest grades would whisper answers to one another, the teacher acting oblivious. Older ones blatantly cheated on exams; to help one another was more important than doing well themselves. Teachers turned a blind eye if it meant their students would succeed. One teacher even asked to see an exam paper of one of her favorite ninth formers in the office of the director; she read it and changed parts so he would pass.

Harold was astonished at the power of threat. He would never want to be part of that! Already in his five years he's seen kids resisting when he pushed too hard. They responded better when he appealed to them to like something, even writing a paper.

Mr. Persons brought up another issue. For years, he'd read essays with names on them. Those from his good students he tended to grade higher; papers from those who did not do well received lower grades. Once when he scored papers using a detailed rubric—each aspect of the paper getting its own score—one of his "weaker" students scored a ninety-seven. The paper itself didn't read particularly well, but each section was nearly perfect.

"I was in a conundrum, a real conundrum. What's a good paper, after all? The rubric system showed me that my personal opinion counted for less. At the same time, I valued my ability to assess thinking and writing. Perhaps I could grade essays without names; I would not be able to incorporate my bias. But I never have; maybe I will before I retire."

The last topic they discussed at the library was more philosophical: the difference between dispensing knowledge and instilling meaning. The push for standardized tests, they both agreed, put emphasis on retaining knowledge, knowledge fit for a time passed. They agreed that state tests did not test for engagement and involvement. They were too broad, too global to have meaning.

"There are so many things I value about my teaching," said Mr. Persons, raising his voice, "things that are not remotely considered in standardized tests. Think about it. I'm concerned about what my students learn, but by no means is that what I care most about. I want them to become resilient, passionate, strong, courageous, creative, empathetic, moral, and have a love of learning. None of these qualities show up on a standardized test. Hence, my distaste."

"I couldn't agree more," said Harold.

"Allow me to share a proverb I learned early in my career. 'I hear and I forget. I see and I remember. I do and I understand.' It has become my guidepost. Whether I taught in a self-contained room, co-taught with colleagues, or worked in a multigrade situation, I've kept this proverb in mind. It has kept me away from succumbing to talk as teaching. Looking for understanding forced me to listen to my students." Harold planned to put this proverb on the cover of his iPad planbook to remind him of priorities.

They both agreed on the futility of drill-and-kill prep for standardized tests, which took time away from instruction and imparted the wrong mind-set. Students get the impression that knowing what others told them was more important than their own search for understanding. Instead, Mr. Persons and Harold Coughlin agreed that teaching well is essential. Keep the focus on involvement and meaning, engage in problem solving, and everyone will be ready for tests. And they agreed that test mania robbed time from the arts, recess, and physical education, which were crucial for becoming educated.

By the time this young teacher left the library, he was feeling better. He could not compete with Snapchatting, but he had more understanding of his role and more tools. He would reconsider how to have his students take more responsibility and how he could better assess their work. He had digital tools, such as Chromebooks, which he would look to discover how they could be effective. And the veteran was grateful for the opportunity to help a young colleague—and be reminded of his earlier years. They agreed to meet again periodically.

NOTES

1. Barbara Ehrenreich, *Natural Causes: An Epidemic of Wellness, the Certainty of Dying, and Killing Ourselves to Live Longer* (New York: Hachette Book Group, 2018), 75.

2. Rosamund Stone Zander and Benjamin Zander, *The Art of Possibility* (New York: Harvard Business School Press, 2000), chapter 3, "Giving an A," 25–53.

3. Ibid.

4. Jon Saphier and Robert Gower, *The Skillful Teacher: Building Your Teaching Skills* (Carlisle, MA: Research for Better Teaching, 5th ed., 1997), 320–22.

Chapter 8

Co-Teach with a Master Teacher
Del Goodwin and Lewis Denton

He would be the director of his own show, a big open door, a chance to discover what kind of teacher he was.

And he was only in his second year.

Lewis Denton considered himself lucky. As he was setting up his classroom, a man, looking like a professor with wisps of hair on his temples and wireless glasses, walked in wearing a gray tweed jacket, white shirt, bowtie, and L. L. Bean moccasins. He spoke in a voice as soothing as rain. "Hello, Lewis. I'm Del Goodwin, department chair. Welcome."

"Nice to meet you, sir," replied Lewis.

By the end of their brief conversation, Lewis learned that Mr. Goodwin had been at the high school for nearly twenty years and department chair for the last five. But most surprising, he had assented to Mr. Goodwin's offer to co-teach Lewis's seniors. Lewis already figured that many of them might be Tom Sawyers hungering for their last day in June, and in his first year and only twenty-two years old, they would most likely try to take advantage of his being a neophyte.

His other four classes were ninth-grade history. As with his fellow new teachers, he expected to close his door and be on his own from the first day. He would sink or swim, hoping not to be one of the 50 percent of new teachers who quit within five years. He'd wanted to be a teacher since his freshman year in college. Once he signed a contract, he was ready—he hoped.

Some of his fellow graduates had mentors, veterans who would stay close to them. They would conference with their protégé, before and after school, over lunch, and during a free period if they shared one. Lewis thought that would be better than nothing. Now he was going to teach alongside a veteran, something he never imagined!

Near the end of his first year, Lewis became convinced that co-teaching with a veteran should be an option in all schools. He thought about encouraging his fellow new teachers to seek such a relationship. Had Lewis been on his own, particularly with disinterested seniors—his school did not state it had tracking, but it might as well have—he may have thought about quitting.

His work with his four freshman sections was easier, but he realized it was in part because of Mr. Goodwin, who would drop in and offer observations and suggestions. Lewis had someone at his back. At department meetings, he gave Lewis broad responsibilities.

Some evenings Lewis took time to write in his journal. He understood that he was privileged to work alongside a master teacher. In a spring entry, he wrote:

> What have I discovered about good teaching?
>
> It's about being willing to *ask big questions*: Don't mess with asking for known information. Choose to ask questions that demand thinking; invite minds to explore and discover. Failing to do this, we shortchange their education.
>
> It's about *addressing attitude*: Don't treat students as cutouts, as shallow figures who simply pass through. Invite them to share themselves, who they are becoming. Let them know that what they think and feel counts. No better place to have this happen than in a classroom.
>
> It's about *giving respect*: Each student comes into the room as who they are. Respect them for that, even if you don't "approve" of them. Let your respect guide them to become good persons.
>
> It's about *acknowledging change*: The best laid plans—each lesson for that matter—morphs the moment it touches others. The more open we are, the more we listen and pay attention to ideas, hopes, and fears, the better the lesson becomes. In my schooling, I had professors who dictated lectures that never touched—except for our pens to take notes. We don't want that.
>
> It's about *seeking discovery*: I like Parker Palmer's, "We teach who we are."[1] We get here through a process of discovery. As a child, we don't know who we will become. We think we are in charge only to discover we are not. Invite our students to discover, to be open to possibilities.
>
> It's about *affirmation*: Nothing slows life more than suppression, foisting doubt, undermining efforts; a teacher who does this to his or her students limits potential. Offer affirmation for good work, for good behavior, for self-respect, for treating peers well.
>
> And it's about *relationships*: In the end, we let students know we care about them. We listen. We connect. Without caring relationships, classrooms can become battlegrounds. They become empty.
>
> I know I will discover more.

At a meeting in the early spring, Mr. Goodwin turned to Lewis and out of the blue said, "I want you to develop a new Asian area studies course in the eighth grade, focusing on China, Southeast Asia, and India. It needs to be dynamic and exciting. This course will be perfect for you. It will set the tone for the department."

Having been asked was enough for Lewis. He would be "moving down" to the junior high, but it would be his course. He would be the director of his own show, a big open door, a chance to discover what kind of teacher he was. And he was only in his second year.

It was then that Lewis decided to write an email letter to his fellow graduate school colleagues about his good fortune co-teaching with Del Goodwin:

Dear Friends,

Something unexpected happened to me before the opening of school. My department head, Del Goodwin, asked if he could co-teach my twelfth-grade Studies in Democracy. Not expecting such a question, I quickly accepted, as I was apprehensive to say the least about this class—some students were only four years younger than I. And I'd heard that Del Goodwin was well known for being one-of-a-kind in the system.

Let me tell you about him. He is nearly fifty, somewhat bald, wears rimless glasses, and speaks in a soft, assured voice. He's been at the school for nearly twenty years. He has an obvious love for teaching and an incredible mind. It didn't take long for me to discover this about him.

Some people might call him a throwback. He's virtually ignored digital tools. He has an iPhone but only for communication. He uses a Mac at home to prepare materials for class and prefers printouts. He excludes smartphones in the classroom. He interacts face to face, listens to his students' ideas, and shares his. When they have screens in front of them, he feels they are distracted, often fail to engage, and drift away.

At this point you might say to yourself, "I am a twenty-first-century teacher in this digital age. I feel pressure to take advantage that digital devices offer: no need to print out documents but simply send them to phones and tablets. I can have students call people from their phones, on-the-spot research in class. I can use my SMART board to create active interaction with materials, to stimulate discussion, and make all classes and assignments available from home. So what could I learn from this veteran who belongs to the twentieth century?"

I will make my case; you'll have to judge for yourselves. First, from our earliest moments, Del Goodwin has trusted me. I don't think he would have asked me to work with him if he did not see something in me. At least that's how I felt at the time. His trust has allowed me to be me—in my first year not yet twenty-three—and like most of you just out of university. He has seen me make mistakes, fumble lessons, but has never reprimanded, only critiqued. He sees through my flaws and supports me anyway. I do not look over my shoulder anticipating judgment. That's a great freedom especially being new. I think we all need this.

Second, Del Goodwin takes control of his curriculum. Aware of standards, he seems to operate outside them—at least it looks that way. He's put aside the textbook traditionally assigned to the course. Instead, he brings in invented, lively material. For example, instead of using the chapter on economics, Del chose to introduce the stock exchange.

You should have seen our students' faces when he assigned each of them to invest $100,000; in three months we would see who were the best investors. When introducing the unit, he passed out the local paper—the class has a print subscription!—and turned to the investment page and showed them how to read it and decide what stocks they might like to buy. He asked me to handle sample calculations on the board. Embarrassed as I am to write this, I flubbed the math—not my strong suit. Working large numbers on the board proved difficult. Every day for the next three months, we checked portfolios. They were certainly engaged!

An aside, I often feel in Mr. Goodwin's shadow; the young teacher who also wears a tweed sport coat and L. L. Bean moccasins—but not a bowtie. I feel self-conscious when seniors see me as Mr. Goodwin's clone. He's in charge and they know it. I am an adjunct, not necessary for the success of the class. Yet because I'm new and not much older than they, I have much to learn. Interns and residents spend years working with doctors before having their own practice. I've been fortunate to have this kind of opportunity!

Third, Del Goodwin has high standards. In his senior honors class, he requires a research paper due at the end of the spring term. Let me say at the outset that his research requirements exceed what I had to follow in college. He makes it clear that research is an answer to a question or problem using carefully considered evidence; it is not taking down information, piecing it together, and drafting a report. (I would be glad to share a copy of his research manual.)

Back to my point. One of his senior girls decided not to write her paper. She was the daughter of a prominent person in the community who was a member of the school board. Mr. Goodwin told this senior that he would hold up her grade, thus not allowing her to graduate. She tested him; he did not back down. A few days before graduation, she passed in the paper—and graduated. I have no doubt he would have enforced his consequence had she failed to complete the assignment.

Fourth, Del is committed to Jerome Bruner's dictum, "We begin with the hypothesis that any subject can be taught effectively in some intellectually honest form to any child at any stage of development."[2] The more teachers adopted Bruner, he contends, the better the learning. When I understood that moving to the eighth grade did not mean to dumb down my course, I jumped at the chance. The idea that I could discuss Confucian philosophy, Buddhism, and Hinduism to thirteen-year-olds was exciting.

Finally, Del has taught me that every student has potential, that no student should be judged based on first impressions. I've never seen him treat a student as though he could not learn. In the stock-market unit, he has the same expectations for everyone: invest, monitor, reinvest, shift investments as desired. Were you to visit, you'd think it was an honors class.

He introduced me to the work of Carol Dweck.[3] She describes two possible mind-sets that a person can have: a *fixed* mind-set and a *growth* mind-set. Those who have a *fixed* mind-set believe their abilities, personality, and moral character are *fixed*; their responses to circumstances either prove or disprove their worth. Those who have a *growth* mind-set, on the contrary, believe their initial talents, interests, aptitudes, and temperaments can be changed through effort. Every challenge is seen as an opportunity.

Del has taught me to see each student as having potential. But when we say to a kid that she is smart, we may unintentionally be telling her to rest on her laurels. But when we treat her as as a learner, not learn-ed, we give her room to strive. As she is working on a project, commenting on her process is far better than saying "Good work!" That phrase can stop her in their tracks rather than spurring her on. I hope I never forget this! I've put the following mantra on my fridge: "I will see each of my students anew every day. I will encourage them to become their best selves. Every class, every day."

As you can see, none of the qualities I've attributed to Del Goodwin relate to a digital classroom. He is old school. But I feel that his ideas can help us. Several of you have indicated via email that you are struggling to engage your "screened-in" kids, who are reluctant to participate in class without having their digital comforts nearby. Del Goodwin has shown me how to be present, to be in relationship through engaging material, and to care about students and what they can do.

I use the iPad for collaborative work—our school has them on carts—and I know the iPad's familiarity is comforting to them. I occasionally have had them use their phones to make directed inquiries during class, but I'm not sure about this idea. Otherwise, phones remain turned off in cubbies by the door. But this year with Del—we'll have one more year—has taught me about trust, about owning my material, having high standards, enacting interactive pedagogies, and respecting each student's potential—and that I should look for it every day.

I hope that all of you are having a good end to your first year. I would love to hear your reactions to my unique situation, to its potential impact on us young teachers. And, to hear about the good stuff that's happened to you.

Sincerely,
Lewis

Several of Lewis's fellow teachers responded to his letter. Most indicated their envy at his good fortune and admitted that it was unlikely to happen in their schools. Lewis was gratified and encouraged them to come visit him.

NOTES

1. Parker Palmer, *The Courage to Teach: Exploring the Inner Landscape of a Teacher's Life* (San Francisco: Jossey-Bass, 1998), Introduction, 1. A profound book on reflecting on the meaning of teaching.

2. Jerome Bruner, *The Process of Education: A Searching Discussion of School Education Opening New Paths to Learning and Teaching* (New York: Vintage, 1960), 33. A small paperback well worth reading.

3. Carol S. Dweck, *Mindset: The New Psychology of Success* (New York: Ballantine Books, 2006, 2016). One of the seminal books for educators.

Chapter 9

Teach Collaboratively

Paula Ralston, Jennifer Symons, and Jeremy Wilson

> *"You're quite right," said the elephant. "Everything must, in one way or another, go. One does what one is wound to do."*

Jeremy Wilson, who was in his second year, was intrigued with Lewis Denton's description of his co-teaching. They'd been to graduate school together. Wanting to document his first year as a member of a three-person collaborative team, he decided to write Lewis and copy the other recipients to his letter.

Dear Lewis,

Your letter touched me. Working with a master veteran! I think of all the ideas and methods you must be learning, certainly faster than you would have on your own. For nearly two years at my middle school, I've been collaborating with two veteran teachers. We are responsible for sixty fifth–sixth graders in three connected classrooms. We work elbow-to-elbow throughout the day, hardly taking a break. We are responsible for the academic curriculum and some electives. Like you, I never expected to have such an opportunity, but I jumped at the chance. I remember learning about John Dewey's progressive methods and the British open-classroom initiatives in graduate school.

You may remember in ed. philosophy how I railed against the formal structure of American schools. In one of my papers, I distinguished the liberating teacher from the credential teacher. Remember?

> For the *credentialed* teacher, credentials are the most significant, perhaps the only requirement for becoming competent. He, or some other authority, determines what is taught. He is a proponent of a prescribed curriculum with

grouping based on standardized tests, and in essence, requires no commitment from him—just compliance.

The *liberating* teacher is more challenging to define. She finds it difficult to conform and function. She consistently urges her students to determine for themselves what they want to learn. A child's concerns become her curriculum; in essence, teaching is an invitation, and if people are not interested in sharing learning experiences, she does not teach.

Sometimes I think I was extreme in my views. My conclusion to that same paper:

> The dominance of traditional education methodology in American public schools must be terminated. This system has failed, and because of its rigid structure, it is incapable of adapting to present demands. Subversive efforts, while moderately successful so far, are beginning to gain momentum. If teachers pursue liberating alternatives with integrity, the potential for successful large-scale subversion may improve.

Unfortunately, my idea of subversion, alas, may not take, at least not now. But I see teachers who exemplify both descriptions. A number of veteran teachers in my school talk at their kids. It's as if they are responsible for delivering knowledge rather than engaging learning. They have their credentials and that's enough. I, on the other hand, have been working in an environment that centers on students. We do not focus on what we teach but on what our students are learning. I did much better in classes when my teachers taught this way.

That I'm in a fifth–sixth grade team with two other teachers at my public school is unusual. This arrangement is a remnant of open-classroom days that began over fifty years ago. When the movement faded, a few teachers persisted to exemplify basic open-ed values: making choices and learning by doing. Somehow, the team survived—and I am fortunate to have this opportunity. We do much more than the traditional four subjects. I and my two colleagues, Jennifer Symons and Paula Ralston, restructured the team a year ago.

Jennifer came from a middle-school math classroom, having taught for ten years. She is well-known for her sense of humor, her passion about teaching, and her collegiality. Paula has been a teacher of multiple subjects at the upper elementary level for more than twenty years. She is well-known for her mastery of different disciplines, her kindness to children and their parents, and her desire to innovate. They have welcomed me into their classroom. Together we are fully responsible for what happens in our three rooms. Parents choose to have their kids in our alternative.

On the wall in our assembly area, Paula has posted a quotation from David Hawkins—one of the gurus of the open-education movement—what has become our philosophy:

> A fundamental aim of education is to organize schools, classrooms, and our own performance as teachers in order to help children acquire the capacity for significant choice, and that learning is really a process of choice.[1]

In a letter to parents in which Paula quoted Hawkins, she included three paragraphs that mean a lot to me:

> [From Paula] As teachers, we are responsible for setting proper limits and conditions from which sensible outcomes may develop. Assignments are an important ingredient in the process, not as commonly prescribed pathways designed to determine students' learning but as starting points toward responsible decision making. We believe that choice is not a privilege but a right—a right we need to teach.
>
> Our main objective is to create a purposeful disciplined classroom. We provide sensible activities to encourage quality work in an atmosphere of mutual respect and support. We implement our curricula on the basis of our students' interests, needs, and requirements.

> [Quoting from Hawkins] We cannot lay out in advance a track that children are going to follow because we don't yet know the things we will learn by observing them which will cause us to make decisions which we haven't thought of. . . . Suddenly, there it is. The bird flies in the window and that's the miracle you needed. . . . If the bird coming in the window is just a nuisance you don't deserve it, and in fact it never happens. If you deserve it, the bird will fly in the window or there'll be a door that opens into the jungle. There will be some romance around the corner that will be there to be captured.[2]

You can see we have a clear idea of our philosophy and purpose—and a feel for the magic of teaching. You also can glean from these writings that we put children first. Each child knows we care about him, his learning, his growth, his well-being—so far from being teachers who dictate curriculum on unsuspecting children. I feel very fortunate to work in this paradigm.

I warn you, Lewis, this may be a long attachment to my email. I've been intending to document what we do. Most of our success has been nondigital. But we do use tablets, have a SMART board in one room, but do not allow smartphones, which are stored turned-off in cubbies.

Paula, Jennifer, and I have spent time discussing the impact, stress, and applicability of the screen in our children's lives. We've noticed the role that apps have in controlling them, such as Marco Polo and House Party video chat rooms; Yellow and its potential false-profile dangers; After School, Sarahah, and Monkey, and anonymous apps; and the most popular, Snapchat. However, the most insidious in our opinion is the Chinese app, Meitu. See Meitu's claims on their website for yourself:

> Meitu is the perfect app to customize your pictures—beautify yourself and your friends, add text, add eye-catching effects to key parts, wipe off what you don't want to show, retouch tiny parts, and so much more. . . . Adjust your facial features to the way you want, just like magic. . . . Instant beatification feature gives you flawless skin, sparkly eyes, straightened nose, etc. in just ONE click! . . . Body shape—ever thought of getting skinnier and taller? Do it with Meitu![3]

The last thing we want for our kids is for them to think they have to manipulate how they portray themselves. We want them to be who they are, warts and all. It may be a losing battle, but we're not giving up. We do not intend to replace parental responsibility, but we can develop awareness and make a positive difference. Almost all the time we stay face to face in interactive learning.

Back to how we are structured. Let me describe our three rooms: The biggest—a former kindergarten space—is for collaborative activities, such as drama, cooking, science, discussions, small-group work, and assemblies; the room next door is for the arts: painting, printmaking, clay, drawing, bookmaking, computer animation, digital processing, and reading aloud; the third across the hall is the quiet room for reading, writing, thinking, word processing, and final product preparation. You would find us and our assistant at any time in any of the rooms; the reading-writing area requires the least supervision.

We are aware of standards and the end-of-the-year testing, but we don't pay much attention to them. Our parents understand that our classrooms are about having the children make choices and do the learning. We do not separate by grade but prefer they group themselves. We offer small-group instruction either to help those who are struggling or to lure them to try something new. And we do not prioritize academic subjects over the arts. Children can choose to paint first thing in the morning and do their math after lunch. Our job is to encourage them to make choices in all areas, stick with them, and get good results.

The children arrive at eight o'clock. Many of them resume activities they'd been working on while others take time to collect themselves. At eight-thirty, we gather our home groups, each in a different room. We set a positive tone for the day: make announcements, point out new opportunities, and share accomplishments. Occasionally, we gather all sixty in the assembly area to watch a student play, hear a guest speaker, hold an all-team meeting, or watch a video.

Near the end of the day, we gather again by home groups. It's time to listen to concerns, share student work, and to simply be together. If need be, we check planbooks, the map of their intentions and attainments for each week. It's also a time to read aloud, a long tradition in our team. Kids are facile with the visual but have had less practice listening. I believe, Lewis, that it's more important than ever.

One of our favorite books has been Philip Pullman's *His Dark Materials* series. Right now we are beginning *The Golden Compass*.[4] Once into a story, they look forward to each episode; already they're intrigued with the heroine, Lyra. Recently I discovered Russell Hoban's *The Mouse and His Child*.[5] It's an older book but rich in imagery, imagination, and vocabulary. I like Hoban's attention to detail.

Early in the first chapter, children hear "blue velveteen trousers," "patent leather shoes," "glass-bead eyes," "white thread whiskers," "black rubber tails." And they see a mouse and his child: "Around and around they danced gravely, and more and more slowly as the spring unwound, until the mouse father came to a stop holding the child high in his upraised arms."[6]

Our conversation began by wondering aloud why these two spin around, what might happen to them, and why the child ends high in the air. Hoban never lets up. Later he introduces a fortune-telling frog, a play on the stage of the Caws of Art, and the lurking Manny Rat.

One more taste, Lewis. Imagine the conversation after hearing this paragraph:

> "You're quite right," said the elephant. "Everything must, in one way or another, go. One does what one is wound to do. It is expected of me that I walk up and down in front of my house; it is expected of you that you drink tea. And it is expected of this young mouse that he go out into the world with his father and dance in a circle."[7]

We often feel pressure to be more like other classrooms. Sometimes, it's difficult being an outlier. But we are fortunate, as I've said, to have strong parental support. And the administration understands the place in history of this alternative. As for me, I could not be more thrilled. I am fulfilling—I hope—my ideal to become a liberating teacher. And I work with two remarkable and supportive colleagues.

Lewis, as I share more, imagine yourself as a child in our classrooms, our active decision-making environment, one without smartphones, where we've convinced parents they do not have to contact their kids directly; instead call the office, what our parents used to do.

We operate without a timetable. We design long periods of uninterrupted time to allow children to become engaged. Of course, some have difficulty, but we persist. Once we conclude our morning meetings, children head to their choice of activity. At 11:00 a.m., some leave for band practice, others for Spanish. We have lunch/recess at the regular time, a chance to mingle with others in the school.

Paula showed me how uninterrupted time allows for deeper involvement in work. The writing is richer as children stick with their thinking, writing, and rewriting. For example, a topic she suggested—"Boys are . . . Girls are . . ."—brought remarkable results.

> "Girls are ones to show boys that they aren't sissy and wear dresses all the time . . . that's the girl I like to be . . . ones who don't mind bugs or worms . . . rough, sporty, full of energy . . . doesn't mind getting filthy dirty in the mud. . . ."
>
> "Girls are the nicest thing that happened to people. Even when they're sitting in mud, throwing a tantrum, or writing on walls with lipstick, they can still avoid a spanking with one innocent look. . . ."
>
> "I like being a boy because I like cars; motorcycles; guns; sports like football, soccer, tennis. . . . Girls like to play dolls, hopscotch, jump rope, and draw horses. . . . When girls take a shower, they take forty-five minutes and come out looking like a just-cooked lobster."
>
> "In the summer, boys go out to dig worms and grubs and go fishing, but the girls stay and play with dolls . . . stare out the window . . . but others come out and play ball with the boys . . . ride bicycles and play hopscotch."

We have lots of other examples of writing, much of it self-directed, to show you if you come. One area that I had some impact in was the clay table. Because the self-hardening clay was being wasted with kids making cups, saucers, dogs, and cats—and not looking much like them—I posted new guidelines: (1) use enough clay to fit in one hand; (2) do not make a recognizable object, such as a cup and saucer or animal; and (3) create an abstract shape with at least one hole.

The result was a series of remarkable sculptures. An unexpected dividend was one student's discovery of wetting a sculpture and rubbing with polished rocks to create a faux glaze; children rub while sitting quietly or listening to stories. Unwittingly, we built a meditation practice into the classroom. We displayed their gray abstracted figures on red velvet as a mini-sculpture garden. Sarah wrote in a letter to me recently:

> Molding clay by hand. Polishing it with smooth stones. This is one of my favorite things to do. Through this, I've discovered that there isn't any right and wrong, when it comes to art, it's how it feels, sounds, smells, looks. It's all about

what's pleasing to you. It also helped define who I am. I look at life as an ever-changing piece of clay. I find beauties in gifts Mother Nature gives us. I create works of art that please my soul.

One of the dangers of a learning-by-doing, creating a making-individual-choices classroom, is the potential loss of community. Our home groups, assemblies, and special events counteract this, and we have whole-team activities. Jennifer told me about her Civil War battlefield role-play that she did last year with all sixty children in the gym. I asked her if she would write a brief account of that day. I've included it here:

> Our Battle of Gettysburg's Blue-and-Gray Generals poised their infantries on their respective half of the floor: soldiers, battalions, and artillery.
>
> I stood at the midline of the "battlefield," in my hand a set of cards. I shuffled them and turned over the first one and said in a loud voice, "Move: take two steps to the left"; every combatant on both sides acted as instructed before the game and took two steps to the left. If enemy soldiers bumped into one another, they fell to the floor, dead. If two battalions—two soldiers or more—collided, the one with the most soldiers survived, the others fell dead. If equal battalions from different sides met, they took two steps back from each other ready for another round.
>
> I read aloud another card: "Still: artillery, shoot." A soldier mimicking a cannon lobs a large wad of newspaper and if it hits soldiers or a battalion, they fall dead. Other cards included: "Move: take three steps forward." "Move: take one step backwards." "Still: artillery shoot." The battle ended when one side had no troops standing.
>
> Our Civil War battlefield was a simple version of what gamers call LARP, or "live action role-play." Ours was live action, yet not sophisticated. Still, the event proved intense. I can still see, Jeremy, the intensity of the faces of the generals as they helplessly observed their troops. When we debriefed, it was obvious everyone had been engaged. They sensed the futility of war, its loss, even the meaning of a pyrrhic victory. We may not have recreated Gettysburg, but it was far better than dodgeball!

Think of the imagination needed to do this, Lewis. The engagement of the battle, the moves, the cannons, the combatants conflicts, the sense of victory, the smell of defeat. And the conversations that followed. No one missed being on their phones!

You may have noticed the recent resurgence of board games. One of my favorites is Diplomacy,[8] a World War I game originally designed for two-to-seven players played in four-to-five hours. With Jennifer and Paula's encouragement, I transformed it into a team-wide activity involving more than twenty students, which lasted six weeks.

Nearly all actions happened in class: negotiations occurred in the open or secretly. I considered allowing smartphones but decided against it; texting avoids interacting. Most would use phones at home in preparation for coming to class. Not much I could do about that—and why should I? It's their communication tool of choice.

Each of the game's seven European Great Powers had two or three "diplomats." They made plans, set up conferences, sent messages, established alliances, wrote articles, created posters, negotiated open and secret contracts, and prepared for moves on the board at specifically announced times: two moves each year, beginning in 1901, one in spring, the other in autumn.

Diplomacy's special quality is its absence of luck—no dice or spin-wheels. Throughout the six weeks, all three rooms showed evidence of play. A French propaganda poster in large letters, "Beware of the Hun"; a poster from Italy, "Don't Trust King Edward VII"; diplomats conferred, sometimes in a room, sometimes in the hall, anywhere they could, and they made public declarations. Before school, after school, at lunch, at home, nearly at any time, in and around their other classwork they negotiated, propagandized, and made open and secret deals.

Treaties made, treaties broken. Secret alliances formed, sometimes held, often quelled. Suspicions surfaced among trusted allies. Diplomats agreed, then turned on each other. Open alliances posted. Tension reigned at each move. It was tense, often drawing in bystanders. I was lucky to be the gamemaster. As I read out moves, diplomats advanced or retreated their armies and fleets on the board—and removed those defeated. Once a Great Power secured eighteen supply centers, it was considered in control of Europe and was the winner.

After the game was over, the class held a Diplomacy lunch, in which children designed a menu based on different European cuisines including French, Italian, English, German, and Russian. The cooks prepared the food in the kitchen and servers set tables with tablecloths and candles. Everyone participated. The celebration was a rousing success; a great community activity.

And those who played interacted—argued, plotted, dealt, whispered, announced—much more engaging than receiving and passing on information on cellphones. In devising plans and plotting to implement them, they dealt with emotions. By the time play was over, you would never think that they'd been screen-centered kids reluctant to have such intense personal interactions as they did in those six weeks. And their language usage became richer.

Although Paula and Jennifer have been in the team longer, we are colleagues. We have a mutual respect, so necessary for success. We meet every day before and/or after school to debrief and plan. When we disagree, we make it a point to find common ground and develop compromise. And I've learned to suppress my ego.

Our planning model is unique. Rather than each one of us taking responsibility for certain subjects, Paula proposed that in place of the traditional delineations by subject matter we should view ourselves as partners in a three-sphere paradigm: initiating/designing/implementing (I/D/I), each essential in an informal teaching setting. Here's a brief description of each sphere:

- *Initiating*: deciding to do something, developing ideas for activities, determining content, deciding a theme, listening to ideas and suggestions, meeting the needs of others—especially students, setting goals, establishing priorities, and dreaming.
- *Designing*: developing spaces, materials, resources, motivators, simulations, activities; organizing experiences; determining sequences; engaging outside persons and resources; setting standards; establishing groupings; integrating with and relating to other areas; developing presentations, demonstrations; and assigning procedures and routines.
- *Implementing*: delivering, critiquing, editing, listening, supporting, helping, observing, following-up, monitoring, assessing, diagnosing, selecting, talking, supervising, teaching, and doing.

We see these spheres as essential and equivalent. A well-designed idea, which does not connect, will fail. So too, initiating a good idea without good design will not work. We like this approach because we are free to take initiative in any area. Paula is particularly good in science, but she's come up with good ideas for writing; Jennifer prefers mathematics but came up with the idea for the Diplomacy banquet. In essence, I/D/I frees us to make choices about teaching, similar to the way we ask our students to make choices about their learning. Collaboration, after all, needs trust.

We rarely give assignments. Our rooms are invitations to explore, probe, think, and do. Displays invite, suggest, and query, like the one that resulted in writings about boys and girls. The rooms are aesthetically pleasing: carefully arranged furniture, plants in the windows, and children's work on walls to surround their minds with possibilities. At home group, we share work from children, point to topics they could explore, and encourage them to pursue initiatives or take on new challenges.

We take time to contact parents. Each quarter, we publish a newsletter indicating what the children have accomplished and what we intend to offer for the upcoming term. We have periodic evenings in which we "teach" parents what we do, and we invite them to plays, musical performances, or to have conversations about teaching in the digital age—the most popular topic.

Finally, we've made sure to have a strong relationship with administration. Both principals visit often, come to some of our planning meetings, and evening events. We believe it's important to work together. After all, we are in the business of improving the lives of children, and both of our principals have offered good suggestions.

I recognize that most teachers who read this description of our collaborative team will consider it far out. I did, too, at first, but I've documented this year in hopes of providing inspiration for thinking anew about how to reach today's digitally driven kids. The more time we spend engaging them in everything from writing to the arts to science tells me they are hungry for engagement, for meaning, for purpose. We find, too, inviting children to solve problems and work collaboratively is preparing an important mind-set for the future workplace.

A world that invites us to pay attention to digital devices that promise ease, happiness, and satisfaction often separates us from each other. I hope that you will explore some of the ideas that I've shared to enrich your classrooms. Let me know what you discover.

And thank you, Lewis, for opening up a dialogue about what matters. Your co-teaching with Del Goodwin and my collaboration with Paula Ralston and Jennifer Symons are but two ways to improve schools. I hope that I can come to see you work with Del; you are certainly welcome to come here. Paula, Jennifer, and I would welcome your observations. And I think it would be a good idea once a month to gather fellow new teachers from the area to have discussions about our work—and invite veterans, too!

My best to you,
Jeremy

NOTES

1. David Hawkins, *The Informed Vision: Essays on Learning and Human Nature* (New York: Agathon Press, 1974), 83–84.
2. Ibid., 93–94.
3. https://mt.meipai.com/en/.
4. Philip Pullman, *The Golden Compass* (New York: Alfred A. Knopf, 1996).
5. Russell Hoban, *The Mouse and His Child* (New York: Harper and Rowe, 1967).
6. Ibid., 2.
7. Ibid., 6.
8. "Diplomacy" (Games Research, 1961).

Chapter 10

Embrace Controversy
Martin Oldenberg, Ellen Harper, and Isabella Gonzalez

> *I drop a single BB into a large metal bowl. . . . This represents "Little Boy," the atomic bomb that destroyed Hiroshima, an area as large as our county.*

Ellen Harper, demure, in a maroon sweater and grey skirt, her blue eyes sparkling and her brown hair in a ponytail, stood spellbound at her door on the first day of school. A hurricane of teens blew in, some darted past, others twisted their necks to check her room number, a few stepped in gingerly. At the bell most were sitting at a desk, a few looking for an open one. She closed her door, stepped to the front, and said, "Hello, I'm Ms. Harper, and this is ninth-grade history. Welcome."

She took attendance that first day, and because she wanted to know their names as soon as possible and for them to know each other's, she made it a priority. She looked at the boy in the first seat by the window, "Bobby—"

"How'd she know my name?" he whispered.

"Please state your name and your favorite thing to do." She then asked the girl in the second seat to state her name—Janet—and repeat Bobby's information and add hers.

The same for the third, George, who repeated Bobby and Janet's information, then offered his. Onto the fourth, fifth . . . onto the next row until the last student in the fifth row, who recited everyone's name and information as best he could. Ms. Harper took her turn but missed a few.

Within a few days, she knew all the names, but she was overwhelmed with her lessons. Her students fidgeted, slouched, often looking down into their laps—at their phones! She'd asked them to keep them in their pocket, but their presence was evident. After school on Friday, she found her new colleague and friend, Isabella Gonzalez, Mexican American, with dark straight hair, tortoise-shell glasses, a flower-patterned dress, and full of energy. She'd been in the department for three years and was respected for her forthright views—despite having annoyed some veterans.

Ellen fretted to Isabella about her students' lack of focus and fixation on their pockets. When she dismissed her classes, nearly everyone would walk out of the room heads down, thumbs on their phones!

"I'm not surprised, Ellen," said Isabella. "I see the same fixation. Unlike the camaraderie we had in my high school in Mexico City, these kids barely interacted with one another when I first taught them. The initial step I took was to build cubbies near the door into which they were to place their shut-off phones. Every phone. They resisted and complained, but I've stuck to my guns. I've broken the first barrier in engaging them, and I have a ways to go, but they no longer have phones in their pockets!

"The next thing I did—now a couple of years ago—was to point out to the department that our curriculum has become outmoded. It was based on textbooks and offered a sequence of courses that was failing to reach kids. It failed to integrate digital tools to make lessons more appealing. I was shocked, Ellen, that our school has only one computer room, only a few SMART boards, and no tablets on carts.

"It was at my insistence that the department reintroduced and expanded on a concept Martin Oldenberg, our senior member now in his last year, formulated over thirty years ago. He called it, 'embracing controversy,' his approach for wrestling with issues. You should talk with him to understand his thinking. We want your course to excite. We know it will be a challenge, but we've invited you to join us because we believe in you.

"Let's go down to Mr. Oldenberg's room. He'll be delighted to speak with you about his ideas, especially his embracing-controversy approach." Isabella paused. "Unfortunately, the department has drifted away from his approach; in fact, from any creative approaches. It seems safer to those in charge to do as their forebears have done: stick to a traditional curriculum, adopt textbooks, stay close to standards, give common exams, and assure that each classroom stays on the same pages in the textbooks.

"Some of us, Ellen are pushing to move away from this pattern but not without resistance. You may not realize it, but we've hired you to help us keep moving ahead. We liked your description of the methods you developed in your student teaching, and I understand that you almost failed because you did not follow protocol. Good for you!" Ellen smiled. She did not know they knew about that.

Ellen and Isabella arrived at Mr. Oldenberg's room. "Nice to meet you, Ellen," he said smiling, his eyebrows raised, crinkling his forehead below his white curled hair. He had the knowing look of a teacher, perhaps a professor, his voice firm and gentle. "Thank you, Isabella, for bringing Ellen.

What can I do for you both?" Ellen explained what she'd told Isabella and Isabella's suggestion that they meet. Mr. Oldenberg agreed to meet on Friday after school at his favorite coffee house, the Blanton. Ellen agreed, looking forward to their conversation.

Martin Oldenberg arrived early at the Blanton, ordered a cappuccino and croissant, and found a corner table. He was anticipating this meeting, as he'd heard that Ellen was special: bright, thoughtful, committed, and not afraid to confront the status quo. He believed she would be a strong addition to the department. He'd heard through the grapevine—so prevalent at his school—that she was making a good impression, and he was equally glad to see Isabella, whom he'd known for three years. He admired her reputation of challenging old ways.

Ten minutes later, Ellen walked in, ordered a green tea, and joined Mr. Oldenberg and Isabella, who'd come with her latte a few minutes before.

Upon meeting Mr. Oldenberg, Ellen wondered if he might be like her favorite social studies teacher in seventh grade. This teacher had done his best to keep Ellen and her classmates off balance; off balance in a good way. He had wanted them to think for themselves, hardly offering his opinions—and he asked great questions.

Once they greeted one another, sharing social niceties, Mr. Oldenberg agreed to tell the story of how his embracing-controversy idea came into being. He was teaching in a new middle school, the social studies person in a four-person team. The school had opened four years before as collection of alternative teams: some traditional, one an open classroom, one an open-schedule format, and another a special-needs team. By the time he arrived, it had reverted to five four-person teams, a close derivation of the former junior high.

"I prided myself being on the fringe. In my first year, the new principal assigned eighth-grade social studies teachers in each team the same paperback texts; she argued that this commonality would prepare students for high school. I did my best to make these texts my own. The economics unit proved challenging but adding role plays helped; the highlight of civil and criminal justice was a mock trial with a local lawyer in his black robe serving as judge, but I found teaching to these texts unsatisfying.

"When a new principal arrived, we were granted more latitude. My team moved to a new area: bigger, more open. I acquired trapezoid tables. No desks! And I was given carte blanche to create my curriculum. It was the 1980s, the Reagan era, the fall of the Berlin Wall, the U.S.–Soviet nuclear arms race, and eventual fall of Communism in the Soviet Union. I wanted to find provocative material to push my students to think, to become involved in issues that mattered. I came up with the concept of 'embracing controversy.'"

As Mr. Oldenberg spoke, Ellen was ready to think how she, too, might take this approach. Her students had no interest in a passive curriculum. Who would want to answer questions at the end of chapters for homework every night? Who would want to learn about something that has no connection to them—and out of a stale textbook! Certainly not her; certainly not them.

Given that she's been asked to improve her ninth-grade course, how would she find issues that would engage? How could she incorporate digital platforms without them becoming distracting? She was ready to listen to this man, famous for being his own teacher.

Mr. Oldenberg took a deep breath. "I want to be up-front with you. I do not pretend to think that my embracing-controversy concept can be transferred to your classrooms. For one, I taught for many years well before standards and testing became the norm; before the impact of digital devices. I was allowed wide latitude in what I taught, so much so that I devised a whole curriculum. And because it was unique, I made it a point to contact parents directly; I wanted them to know what their children were learning in my class.

"So, why am I telling you this? Because I believe that you both—young, twenty-first-century teachers—have more latitude than you may think, and I'm aware that you have end-of-the-year tests to face, tests that may determine the fate of the school. Take these threats—as I see them—away from your minds. Teach as well as you know how. Challenge your kids, involve them in conversations, boost their curiosity, demand good writing, encourage cooperation, and persist. Solve problems together. Don't rely on drill-and-kill test prep.

"Seek ideas from others and use ones that work. I learned a long time ago that I could not do it alone. I sought the advice of those who went before me and from exemplary colleagues—everyone knows who they are. I am grateful that you are asking me to return the favor.

"Early on," Mr. Oldenberg said with a sigh, "I observed that schools wall themselves off from the outside world, fiefdoms protecting their inhabitants. Coming into a school as an outsider was intimidating. This was before 9/11 and the first school shootings when 'protecting' schools had become the norm. And parents' nights did not work for me; they were dog-and-pony shows designed to put the school in a good light.

"Let's talk about parents. Here's an excerpt of a note I wrote to parents in the mid-1980s." He handed Ellen and Isabella a copy:

A Note to Parents about Eighth Grade Social Studies
From: Mr. Oldenberg

Do you think Tsar Ivan IV was crazy?
In *Animal Farm*, why did the pigs post the Seven Commandments?

How come Japanese Americans in Hawaii were not interred during WWII?
Why not arrest every Klansman who wears a robe in public?

Questions, questions, questions—the heart of eighth-grade social studies. I intend to have a classroom where questions and inquiries are more important than answers and conclusions, where respect and deference prevail over insistence and dominance, and where listening and responding are equivalent to speaking and convincing.

I've divided the curriculum into three phases, each to investigate a different topic: (1) Russian geography and Tsarist history, the nuclear threat; (2) George Orwell's *Animal Farm*; and (3) Minorities: Japanese-American internment and the Ku Klux Klan. I will rotate these units through each of the three groups. One unit becomes a database for comparison with another. . . . For instance, knowledge about Tsar Ivan IV of Russia provides a vehicle for comprehending Napoleon's leadership on Animal Farm—and vice versa.

Ellen never heard of contacting parents directly except to conference about their kids. She thought this role was the purview of the administration. She wondered how this approach would work. Perhaps it could be done through email or other electronic medium and could possibly become interactive. But, Ellen wondered, "Would I want this on my plate along with all my other responsibilities? Yet I do like Mr. Oldenberg's list of student expectations that he put in the same newsletter. I intend to adapt them."

Students need to

1. recognize that all issues that matter are complex and require thoughtful, attentive, and balanced consideration
2. assess values and grapple with significant questions as a means to inquiry and learning
3. discuss with intelligence: speak with clarity, listen with care, and express your thoughts and feelings
4. participate in the varied forms of social studies learning including note taking, map work, study guides, letter writing, essay writing, group work, and creative projects
5. experience interdependent learning through cooperation and sharing, yet recognize that you are responsible for your own results
6. realize that your ideas and actions do make a difference both to yourselves and to your classmates

Ellen and Isabella were listening to a veteran who had set up his own curriculum, no reference to standards—there were none. There was no anticipation of external judgment—except a principal's yearly evaluation—and no intention to use the same material with every class at the same time. Ellen wondered if she could structure her classes to have a separate sequence for each. It would certainly make her day less repetitive.

Mr. Oldenberg handed Isabella and Ellen another document. "I've thought a lot about the teaching process," he said. "I never saw it as automatic: doing the same thing day after day. This list is a recent distillation. I hope it will help you."

- Build your teaching from within; don't conform to others' expectations.
- Be willing to open Pandora's Box to discover new possibilities.
- Do not set minimum competencies; instead maximize expectations.
- Teach inside dilemmas, weigh moral issues, and avoid black-and-white dialogue.
- Listen to your students, respect what they think, and care about what they care about.

"Ellen and Isabella, you are models for your students and responsible for their actions. Think about conversations with your students where you see yourself exercising the privilege of sitting at the table with them as fellow human beings. You are the teacher but also a member of a community."

"I realize now," said Isabella, "my preparation has been focused on content and skills; much of it centered around meeting Common Core standards. I've done my best to make my lessons engaging. However, this conversation is pushing me further. I want to apply your principles. How to do it effectively is the question. I'll have to figure out how, as you had to figure things out in your early days."

"I agree with you Isabella," said Ellen. "We should talk more about this."

"Before I describe one of my embracing-controversy topics," Mr. Oldenberg said, "I want to clarify: The success of these ventures depended upon my relationships with students. I discovered early on that they had to know that I would listen to them, that I cared about who they were and what they thought. The trust we developed allowed them to speak out and kept me from making judgments. I spent a lot of time before and after school listening to them. As we entered each controversy, I would hear their ideas and not have to worry about what they thought I wanted to hear. It takes time to build relationships, but it's the only way I can teach."

Mr. Oldenberg then described one of his first embracing-controversy topics: his multiple approaches for elucidating the U.S.–Soviet threat of nuclear war in the 1980s. It had several components:

- Reading aloud Russell Hoban's *Riddley Walker*.[1] Written in an invented language, Hoban's book would be a challenge but easier to understand if

I read it aloud. My students absorbed his description of an almost incomprehensible world. Squirming in their seats at times, they pieced together the subtleties of an unrecognizable people and bleak landscape. Judging from conversations and after-class inquiries, they understood the possible consequences of the nuclear arms race—certainly were more aware. Reading Hoban's masterpiece encouraged me to pursue the issue.

- The next year, I assigned John Hersey's *Hiroshima*.[2] Written in clear, lucid prose, Hersey's book, in 160 pages of unambiguous prose, proved accessible. Hersey narrated the harrowing stories of six survivors: two doctors, a Protestant minister, a widowed seamstress, a young female factory worker, and a German Catholic priest. He wrote an almost matter-of-fact account of their struggles after the bomb. Compassionate, eloquent, Hersey's classic portrayal framed this tragedy perfectly. Reading it today would have a similar impact.

- Graphic, black-and-white, 12" x 18" photographs placed around the room and in the hallway open to my room: I still see some them in my mind—the Enola Gay crew before its historic flight; the skeletal remains of Hiroshima's buildings; and frightening images of survivors. A vaporized shadow of a person on a wall behind a ladder; a woman with a keloid scar on her face—permanent, large, and claw-like; a man's face cluttered with radiation effects; and a survivor with huge keloid scars over his back.

  Placing these images caused concern from teachers and a few parents. They became the subject of a school board hearing. In the end they stayed, but I'm not sure they should have. Today on the Internet, the most graphic of these photos are presented, in Internet-speak, as "images they don't want you to see."

- *Atomic Café*, *The Day After*, and dropping BBs in a metal bowl: I thought it was important to show anti-nuclear-war films. Some of the graphics were tough. However, the BB exercise pushed the envelope. Here's the dialogue I had:

"Everyone, will you please sit here on the floor? Now, please close your eyes. You, too, Jeff. I know it's hard for you. And you, Mike. Okay. Please listen carefully. Everyone be very, very quiet . . . very quiet . . ."

I drop a single BB into a large metal bowl. . . . "This represents 'Little Boy,' the atomic bomb that destroyed Hiroshima, an area as large as our county." After a pause, I drop another single BB. Again quietly, "That's 'Fat Man,' the bomb that detonated Nagasaki, again an area as large as our county."

Another pause . . . I drop ten more BBs, one at a time, very, very slowly: "These represent the amount of hydrogen bombs that could destroy life on earth." After a longer silence, I slowly pour the rest of the one thousand BBs into the metal bowl, taking almost half a minute: "These represent all the bombs that are stored in US and Soviet arsenals."

Sharing this dialogue gives you an idea of the impact of this exercise. Perhaps I should have brought in the bowl and BBs to drive home the point. Had you been there, you would have heard a pin drop in between the harsh sounds of the BBs—and the long silence afterwards. Perhaps I pushed too far. But I had no regrets.

- I did not give tests. Instead, I invited them to write poems, make illustrations, create stories, and write essays and letters. I wanted to find out if my intended objective to explore the threat of nuclear war had reached them. Did they comprehend the realities of that time? Did Hersey's *Hiroshima* connect with them? In the end, did they resist, feel helpless, or scared—or empowered?
- Finally, I read aloud Dr. Seuss's *The Butter Battle Book*,[3] so appropriate then—and now, I think. It's the story of Yooks and Zooks: Yooks who butter their bread right side up, Zooks who butter upside down. They build a wall between them, which starts an arms race threatening mutual destruction. It begins with one patrolman's "Tough-Tufted Prickly Snick-Berry Switch" slingshot and escalating to each side having a "Bitsy Big-Boy Boomeroo." In the end, each side's general is poised to drop their bombs waiting for the other side to strike first.

Ellen raised her eyebrows, "So, how did your students react? Did you realize your expectations? Were they scared? Concerned? Or, as you wondered, empowered?"

Anticipating their curiosity, Mr. Oldenberg handed them a folder with examples of their responses. Opening it, they saw poems, stories, letters, and illustrations. "Take this folder home, both of you, and take a close look at the work. Imagine the kids creating them, kids who were living through the height of the threat of nuclear war, and think about what issues you might include in your classrooms and how you could invite your kids to respond.

"I wanted to know what my students understood, realized, accepted, or rejected. What was prominent in their minds, what mattered to them—not to me—and what they cared about. That was far more important than what a body of tests could reveal. You may think I am preaching, and you'd be right. If I could give the profession a message, this would be one of them!"

Mr. Oldenberg suggested that they look together at a few pieces in the folder. He took out three poems:

Scars.
The city is still partly rubble,
People are living—some not,
But the scars are deep.
 Some visible
 Some invisible
Ugly faces, deformed bodies
Shunned people, polluted people
Left alone after so much pain
So much sorrow
To begin one's life again in a scarred city.

~Sarah

The air is hazy no one around,
all is lost no hope is found,
there's just a shadow
burnt in a wall,
no sign of substance, no sign at all.

~Julie

Life is precious,
Life is grand,
That's why war must be banned.

~Wendy

"Had I given a test, I would never have seen Sarah's vision of the city, revisited Julie's recalling of an image posted on our wall, or heard Wendy's cry for life. I would not have heard their impressions, thoughts, and feelings. They would have studied for the test they expected me to give."

"I've never found writing poetry easy," said Isabella. "It's a form I have difficulty grasping. Still, I can see from these three what was on the mind of each of them. I think I'll be more open to poetry. If I have trouble understanding, I'll come to Ellen who writes her own."

"I'd be happy to help," Ellen said.

"Another piece in the folder was Noah's empathic 'The Day.'" Mr. Oldenberg smiled as he recalled Noah's story of Toshiro Makatsu's eighty-ninth birthday morning. Handing them a copy, he asked Ellen and Isabella to take time to read it.

> Today, at exactly 8:30 a.m., Toshiro Makatsu would be 89 years old. No matter that he was blind. No matter that a war was happening. Today was his birthday, and he was going to do what he wanted, war or no war . . .
>
> After checking his garden, Toshiro, feeling at peace with the world, made his way to one of the low wooden benches carefully interspersed along the garden path. Here he sat and happily listened to the song of a bird, mingled with scents of the flowers in his garden . . .
>
> Soon the sun grew hotter and the bench became uncomfortable. He rose and slowly navigated his way to another bench in the shade of his screened porch.
>
> No sooner had he sat down than a great invisible force picked him up and tossed him with the rubble of his tiny house, back into the garden. It was 8:15 a.m.
>
> Fifteen minutes before his 89th birthday, Toshiro Makatsu passed into history as a statistic, merely one of the 100,000 people who died with him in the same instant.

"And let's look at Noah's preface":

> Forty years later, we know that 100,000 people died at the instant the bomb was detonated. But still, forty years later, that number remains only a statistic. We cannot grasp the enormity of the suffering that took place…There is no way to tell a story about what dying in an instant felt like except through our imagination.

"My goodness, Mr. Oldenberg," said Ellen. "What depth, what understanding—and from a thirteen-year-old!"

"You'll also find in the folder other responses, a letter to the president, and another to the local paper":

- The whole arms race is so ridiculously like a fight between small children, that if it weren't life threatening, it would be almost funny. ~Katie
- The sight of a mushroom cloud is pretty powerful. . . . Even though I know how harmful it is, I still think it is kind of a majestic sight. It's a shame that it has to be so harmful. The thought of the end of life is very depressing for me. ~William
- . . . kiss your life good-bye / if at first it doesn't kill you instantly / what a horrible life your life would then be. . . ./ Your life the bomb stole. ~Sarah
- Lord, forgive us. We have taken your world as you gave it and turned it around. . . . Guide us through the years ahead, or have you backed away? Forgive us, Lord. ~Cathy

Mr. Oldenberg turned to talk about his recent effort to raise controversy. He showed his junior section the 2014 documentary of Sebastião Salgado's work and photographs, *The Salt of the Earth*. Salgado's renditions of wrenching images of war and poverty expressed a human horror as graphic as the Hiroshima photographs that Mr. Oldenberg had shared years ago.

The filmmaker's revelatory eye projected images, which he doubted his students had ever seen despite the omnipresent Internet. No one gagged; perhaps they were more than used to such images and numb to the world's horrors. However, Salgado's documentary ended with "Genesis," a statement of hope and love for the planet. Mr. Oldenberg told Ellen and Isabella that he hoped his nuclear war unit, in the end, gave his adolescents hope for a better future.

"Given what you've told us, Mr. Oldenberg," said Ellen, "you see the positive. Embracing controversy, as I understand it, means looking at issues from the "emperor-is-not-wearing-any-clothes" perspective. If we fail to stay grounded in reality, we will be doing our students and our society a disservice. You have helped me reframe my pedagogy."

It had been nearly two hours. Isabella and Ellen expressed their appreciation of Mr. Oldenberg's time with them. They liked meeting at the Blanton and agreed to meet again.

Ellen wanted to capitalize on Mr. Oldenberg's wisdom. She saw herself taking a path that would invite greater involvement from her students. She wanted nothing to do with passive delivery. Her students deserved much better. And for the next time, she wanted to hear Mr. Oldenberg's thoughts about the widening divide in the national conversation, particularly in light of the Trump–Clinton election and the role of Russian interference.

NOTES

1. Russell Hoban, *Riddley Walker* (New York: Simon & Schuster, 1980).
2. John Hersey, *Hiroshima* (New York: Alfred A. Knopf, 1946).
3. Dr. Seuss, *The Butter Battle Book* (New York: Random House, 1984).

Chapter 11

Teach Reading for Understanding
Carolyn Hench and Lea Archer

You've chosen to grow, not to stagnate. That was one of my mantras: "Don't do tomorrow what I did today." Keep fresh. Be open to surprise. Open to new ideas.

Lea Archer arrived at her new school full of enthusiasm. Animated, energetic, her blonde hair askew, often wearing colorful pantsuits, she had a prevalent smile. She had anticipated becoming a teacher since her senior year in high school. By the end of her first month in the classroom, she found some success but discovered surprising concerns. She decided to seek help. Her colleagues suggested she meet with Carolyn Hench, the former chairman of the department, now retired. Lea emailed her to ask if they could get together. Ms. Hench replied and suggested they meet at the Zebra Café on Saturday morning.

The day came. Lea found Ms. Hench at a table by the window. She looked younger than Lea expected. Her dark gray hair was swept back, a warm smile on her face revealing a gentle demeanor. She was dressed in a dark blue pantsuit. After exchanging personal niceties, Ms. Hench leaned back and mused, "I can imagine you, Lea, in my old second-floor room and wonder how you're doing with your students. I spent many years there, each one different, mostly full of surprises and some disappointments. I hope you will have a good first year. Before we begin talking about this past month, could you tell me, Lea, how you decided to become a teacher?"

"I'll be glad to. In the summer of my sophomore year in college, the dean asked me to care for children of the twenty-fifth reunion class. I was responsible for about twenty-five, except at mealtimes. By the end of the weekend, I'd learned their names—boys and girls six to sixteen—kept them occupied, and relished every minute of it. When I said, 'Who wants to play softball?' like a school of fish, they would follow me.

"No matter what I asked, they complied. I was a pied piper—and loved it! No one told me what to do. I never looked over my shoulder to see if anyone was watching me. I knew then for sure that I wanted to be a teacher. I was being called.

"And I learned a lot from that weekend. If my students were to be good to one another, I had to be accepting and forgiving of myself, something that had been hard for me to do. My commitment to teach became a wake-up call. I would need persistence to succeed. I wanted to evoke memories—to be responsible for what I created. And here I am."

"Good for you, Lea. I could not imagine teaching without being called. It's a challenging profession, full of quirks, surprises, disappointments, and joy. Now that you've been at it for a month, how are you feeling about your choice?"

"I don't know where to begin, Ms. Hench. So much has happened. My poetry course is going pretty well, and kids are responding, but we have a long way to go. Frankly, I don't think I've fully engaged them, but I'm making progress. Many seem distracted and struggle to engage in discussions, but they're getting better. I'm nervous, very nervous, about having to teach Shakespeare's *Hamlet*—I mean *really* nervous. I've never read the play, let alone studied it, and Shakespeare was difficult for me.

"What has struck me in conversations, Ms. Hench, is my students' lack of vocabulary; they speak in shorter sentences. I remember the extended discussions my classmates and I had when I was in school. Sometimes, teachers couldn't shut us up. I wish I had that dilemma. I have to pull teeth to get them to pursue an argument; they seem to have little curiosity. I've discussed this with colleagues and think I've discovered some relevant factors." Lea became more animated as she continued,

"First, my students spend six-to-seven hours a day on their phones. They are away from interacting with one another. Second, they prefer to communicate by texting: multiple short blurbs, emoji, simple information that either disappears or is passed on. Third is the impact of sound-bite television with no restrictions as to truth; think of Fox News. And last, an external factor—mostly applying to adult society—the impact of 140-character tweets (or now 280) as a primary source of information.

"To counteract this digital culture, I intend to form communities in my classroom; no phones, only face-to-face interactions. A friend of mine told me about Yondr, a system that creates phone-free areas. I decided to invest in this system for my classroom. I bought cases for my students' phones to use when they enter the classroom.

"Yondr works like this: As they arrive, they put their phones in a case, and lock it. The phone is shut down. Some still cling to it in their laps, as if they need to have it nearby. When they leave, to retrieve their phones, they tap their cases on an unlocking base. I have suggested to our principal to look into Yondr to make the school a phone-free zone.[1]

"Before I got Yondr, I once asked them to retrieve their phones from the cubbies. I had them read and listen to poetry by Dylan Thomas. We had a conversation about the ones they liked best; some even read aloud. They seem to like that, comfortable having phones at hand, and it improved my cred with them. Perhaps they liked taking initiative with their smartphones rather than the smartphones using them. But the more I think about it, Ms. Hench, the more I realize I have no need for smartphones in my classes. Because even on the day we read Dylan Thomas, some students surfed on their phones for personal purposes."

"A smart observation, Lea. You are addressing issues head-on. I commend you for that. Were I in your position, I'd take similar approaches. I miss the classroom, but I've had my turn. It's your time now. I've been thinking about the current shift in dialogue, not only in school but in the nation.

"To change the subject, here's another idea for you. More than ever, it's important to focus on teaching reading for understanding. Where else will students get this? In reading articles in the paper these days, I've noticed an increasing amount of tweets interspersed. It began with the incessant tweeting of the president and has persisted. I fear tweets will lead to a slow decline of reflective writing. If people only react to tweets and sound-bites, they're deprived of extensive thinking.

"I agree, Lea, about your concern about students' lack of vocabulary, of language usage. I believe this is serious, but you can confront it by emphasizing reading for understanding."

"And, Ms. Hench, I forgot to mention—in addition to the six-to-seven hours my students are on the phone—is the increased amount of time they watch videos, mostly YouTube. Videos, and movies on Netflix and Amazon Prime, are not equivalent to reading a book. The other day, I passed out a two-page opinion piece on the use of metaphor in poetry and watched them struggle to grasp its meaning, let alone form opinions. Its language was not complex, nor were the ideas. They had a hard time making sense of it and discussing the implications. I've noticed, however, since using Yondr, my students are improving; they remain better focused.

"I think back to the 1960s when you were teaching Jane Austen. One of my colleagues told me about the time your students took two class periods to analyze a controversial one-plus-page commentary about her. I couldn't imagine my students taking even half a period to consider it! And without my prodding, would they even attempt to discover its meaning? Not only is their language less sophisticated, but so is their curiosity to learn through reading. I am going to make this one of my missions, as a well-informed public is necessary in a democracy. I want to do my bit."

"You are taking the right road, Lea. I've seen the effect of the sound-bite culture—and unfortunately its power: tweets and tweets in the print world, *Fox News*'s evening shows on television, and a plethora of faux-Internet sites. People seem willing to accept what they first hear without considering implications. They barely spend more than ten seconds on sites when surfing.

"Because of the Internet's accessibility and Google's instant searches, they become accustomed to accepting what they find as quickly as they find it. How many of us, for instance, go beyond Google's first search page? Social media tends to quicken information acquisition, and the ease of texting lures us away from reflection, as it happens quickly."

"I intend to attack this problem on multiple fronts, Ms. Hench. First, I will ask what I call curiosity questions, ones that do not have simple answers. Such questions as, 'When will the world end?' 'Why would we try to be better without first trying to be good?' 'What is the color of a mirror?' 'Where is the center of the universe?' I intend to pursue answers with 'why.' Sometimes, I will invoke 'the-why-five-times' approach, which I learned from a friend, to get them to dig more deeply; it's an amazing process. Most curiosity questions will be random—but I'll try to include some that address current content.

"And I intend to give homework that makes them think and perhaps to ask their parents and others for opinions. No rote worksheets. Sometimes I will give them short readings that they'll need to interpret in their own words or invite them to draft a précis of an article. I know that working at home may be difficult for some, so I won't punish those who can't manage. I also intend to find reading material that's not only provocative but accessible. I'll persist with multiple questions that get at meaning, and at times, I'll place them in groups of three to develop a consensus position on an issue, then articulate it to the class.

"I hope this process will inculcate a sense of the power of asking, of figuring out, of knowing, and sharing what they know. Knowledge is power—but it has to be honest. No alternative truths allowed.

"I have become a fan of Krishnamurti since my educational philosophy professor in graduate school introduced him. My favorite quotation, which I carry in my purse is this—let me read it to you: 'Intelligence is the capacity to perceive the essential, the *what is*; and to awaken this capacity, in oneself and others, is education.'[2]

"Krishnamurti's wisdom in his *Education and the Significance of Life* convinced me—if I had any doubts—that to be a teacher is truly a noble calling. What more could I do for my kids than to have them see the world as it is? Yet how difficult to do in these times when the 'world' keeps telling them what it is; the Internet bombards them, as does social media. I hope my classroom will be a welcomed respite, a chance to step back and see society for what it really is. If I don't do that, my students will become susceptible to the will of others. I intend to show that I care about each of them and what they think and have to say."

Lea was on a roll. Ms. Hench's feedback opened doors. She was delighted to tell her about Krishnamurti—and pleased that Ms. Hench also liked the book. "How wonderful to speak deeply about teaching!" thought Lea. She hoped that Ms. Hench and she would have many opportunities to explore ideas. And Ms. Hench was thinking how lucky Lea Archer's students were.

"Back to classroom approaches, I have another idea," Lea said. "When I assign a book and then show a movie, I intend to help my students to see similarities and differences. I'm thinking of asking questions in both instances. After each chapter of the book, I would ask, 'How do you see the main characters? What words describe your feelings? Is one of the characters the antagonist? What images remain with you? And what does the book make you think about in your life?'

"For the movie, at intervals while showing it, I'll ask similar questions. Once done, I will ask students to write how they see each as similar and different, then share their conclusions and follow with a discussion. The main purpose will not be to determine which medium is better but for them to see that each has value. Finally, I will ask, 'What if we lived in a society with only movies and no books? Would it make a difference?' Can you think of other approaches, Ms. Hench?"

"You're on to something, Lea. No doubt, as you pursue these ideas, you'll make adjustments and come up with others. You seem dedicated to improve reading literacy—and verbal and visual literacies. You are in the right department. You've chosen to grow, not to stagnate. That was one of my mantras: 'Don't do tomorrow what I did today.' Keep fresh. Be open to surprise. Open to new ideas. An endless process throughout my career.

"And I do have a suggestion: What about invoking role plays? Have students take on the role of a character in either film or literature. Have them develop monologues advocating their part. Follow up with other students acting as reporters who interview characters to get at their motives, intentions, and desires, and have the characters crosstalk to bring up issues, concerns, likes, and dislikes. Have the reporters write their impressions as news articles and have the characters write letters to another character in the film or book. These are some ideas off the top of my head. I hope they suggest something for you.

"And before we leave today, Lea, I want to share some more thoughts. In my heyday, I needed to prod students to read for understanding. Simply to assign a book, particularly one without spice and violence, I had to make an extra effort if I wanted to hear what they thought. I did not tell them what they should understand; that would keep them from seeing the 'what is' of the book for themselves. I've brought excerpts of what I wrote to my students before assigning Alexander Solzhenitsyn's *One Day in the Life of Ivan Denisovich*.[3] The first quotation puts reading it in perspective":

> It is on the edge of life where we discover the most about ourselves. The great spiritual leaders throughout history agree that going into the desert enables us to become in touch with the essentials of life. Ivan Denisovich is the story of a man on the edge, "where a couple of ounces ruled your life." Each moment of his day borders on living or dying, which was true for each and every day in the ten years of his sentence. It is hard to imagine such a life while we sit in the comforts of our classroom. Or the lives of our neighbors who live in poverty in our city.

"I saw my students entering a privileged place being able to read about a man's day in prison, in the gulag for that matter. Before I passed out the books, I gave them a handout":

> Read the book as if you are beside Ivan. Inside his head. Sit with him, eat with him, work with him, breathe with him. Think back to the end of *To Kill a Mockingbird* when Scout reminds herself that "Atticus was right. One time he said that you never really know a man until you stand in his shoes and walk around in them. Just standing on the Radley porch was enough."[4] Though we cannot walk in Ivan's shoes, perhaps we can involve ourselves enough in the story as if we were standing at the fence of the camp. The more you enter into Ivan and the details of his day, the more interesting the read.

"As the years passed, I had to become more convincing to engage reading. I must say, the efforts were worth it. I sometimes hear from my kids how much they appreciated the literature we read.

"Another thought: When I became a teacher, now many years ago, I expected my students to want to be students. Most of them did just that. But as the years passed, more seemed to come with chips on their shoulders. I saw them resisting, avoiding, ignoring—not accepting my overtures. We were out of touch with one another. I asked myself what I could do to bring them into the fold. I decided to shift my thinking. Here's what I wrote to myself, Lea":

> I intend to evoke deep respect and treat my students as honored guests. Accept them as they are and welcome them into a safe learning place. Teach them to take breaths to center themselves. Help them bring focus into their work. Teach them without stress. Enjoy each and every one of my students. Enjoy what we are together.

"Once I developed this 'honored guests' mind-set, I began to see a change. More respect for me, more respect for each other. And more from them as to what they thought. It wasn't perfect, Lea, but things got a lot better!

"And since I've left the classroom, I've been following what's happening in schools. I've observed the impact technology, especially the smartphone. I have one and am amazed at what it does."

"I have one, too," said Lea. "I don't know what I'd do without it. However, I've chosen not to have it beside me in class. I want to focus on my students. Sometimes I think smartphones have become the elephant in the room. But I've been thinking, I need to deal with it head-on with my students. Simply having them put phones away in Yondr cases could avoid having to deal with their power and influence. We all know how addictive they are. It's a different culture from the one in which you and I grew up.

"Because I see the relationship with the phone as addictive, I intend to address its heavy use. My colleagues and I are designing a survey, one that asks how often kids think they check Instagram, Facebook, Snapchat, and other apps during the day. These are other possible questions: Do they sleep with their phones; check them during sports; while watching TV and movies; while sitting at a table with friends; and when do they not rely on them?

"We might include on the survey suggestions for downtime like taking phone sabbaticals, even for a few hours let alone a day. Things like that. We've only begun the process. Perhaps we will help them free themselves from feeding their habit. These phones are addictive. I know, because I have been there!

"At our last faculty meeting, a colleague told us about an article that suggested Apple, in its future phones, help customers become less dependent. The idea I liked was having the phone give a report on how we've spent our time in the past week.[5] I think such awareness can go a long way to living better with our phones."

"I'd like to take your survey," said Ms. Hench. "Let me know when you have it ready."

"I certainly will. Thank you, Ms. Hench for meeting with me today."

"And I want to thank you, Lea, for inviting me into your teaching life. It's an honor to be asked, to have had this conversation."

Lea smiled. She felt she was on a good path. Despite disappointments, in the weeks following each day was getting better. She'd observed different responses to her prodding, noticed more smiles, and saw better posture and greater attentiveness. Lea knew she had a long way before she "got it"; perhaps she may never. But she intended to come as close as she could. She saw herself opening up to her students, becoming more comfortable. As she shed the shell of "teacher," they became more personal with her, her lessons would feel less pull-and-tug and more give-and-take.

She was grateful for her conversation with Ms. Hench, particularly for giving her the green light to become a role model. Without her guidance, Lea suspected she would be less open to taking unmapped roads and would miss the excitement that comes from being creative.

And she was less worried about having to teach Shakespeare's *Hamlet*!

NOTES

1. https://www.overyondr.com. Explore this site for more ideas.
2. J. Krishnamurti, *Education and the Significance of Life* (New York: Harper & Row, 1953), 14.
3. Alexander Solzhenitsyn, *One Day in the Life of Ivan Denisovich* (New York: Signet Classics, 1963).
4. Harper Lee, *To Kill a Mockingbird* (New York: Harper Perennial Classics, 1960), 282.
5. Farhad Manjoo, "It's Time for Apple to Build a Less Addictive Phone," *New York Times*, January 17, 2018.

Chapter 12

Invest in Social-Emotional Learning

George Persons, Harold Coughlin, and Amanda Booker

Don't smile before Christmas break.

Harold Coughlin found his new colleague, Amanda Booker, in the teacher's room after school. They taught English in the ninth and tenth grades. Amanda was already making her mark. Her demeanor was quiet and firm. In the classroom, she'd lean forward with raised eyebrows when listening and frown when needing her students' full attention. Principal Judson spoke highly of her as one of his best young teachers, and students had said how much they liked her. Harold was curious, however, why Amanda had transferred from an inner-city school. The next time he saw her, he'd ask.

Amanda explained, "As much as I enjoyed my former school, I felt I needed more tools to connect with students. Often I found myself at odds with them, even ones who came from my 'hood. They would not take school seriously and would become disorderly. I seemed unable to offer them much. If I could come to a different school, away from my community, I might find good ideas and methods.

"Another reason for wanting to leave was our merging conflict with administration. Because of state and federal pressure to meet standards, and for our kids to pass those darn tests, administrators started to drop into our classrooms with their laptops. They come to the back of the room and type up everything we were doing. Can you imagine how disconcerting that was! We were being pressured to conform rather than encouraged to challenge students to think and form their own understandings. I wanted to be a teacher so that I could engage with kids, have them think, nurture their curiosity, create aspirations, and support their dreams.

"I'll never forget a text I received last spring from a colleague: 'The laptop was last seen on the second floor. Make sure you're on the lesson you are supposed to be on and that what you are teaching matches your "I can" statement. Oh, and make sure you have enough anchor charts hanging on the walls.'

"You'd think we were all lunatics in an insane asylum! Now you can see why I wanted out. How could I create ways to engage kids while having to succumb to this 'laptop' oppression? Administrators might have thought they meant well, but were they to spend time in my shoes they would have realized how far off they were. I already sense in this school that the faculty is taking full responsibility for what they do and how well they do it. I'm grateful to be here."

"That's quite a story," said Harold. "I have an idea, Amanda. Why don't we meet with George Persons? He's a senior member of the English department in his last year. I've talked with him before and learned a lot. We've spoken mostly about grading. His ideas have given me a new perspective, which I will share with you. Meanwhile. I'll arrange a meeting."

A week and a half later, Harold and Amanda found Mr. Persons at a back table at the town library where he and Harold had previously met. After exchanging greetings and hearing why Harold brought Amanda, Mr. Persons put down his newspaper and leaned back in his chair.

"It sounds like, Amanda, from what you and Harold have told me, you have a good handle on content, a cornerstone of a good classroom." And you certainly faced challenges in your former school. Let me share an insight I came to after only a couple of years teaching. I had more success when I focused on forming good relationships with my students. I made that integral to my lessons, not as a separate curriculum. And I encouraged them to become more self-aware, which is not an easy task. Young people tend to see others controlling their lives rather than seeing themselves as causal agents.

"As a student teacher in an inner-city school, my master teacher whispered to me in front of my first class, 'Don't smile before Christmas break. That way, they will know you mean business. And the first opportunity you get, send one of the good girls, preferably one who wears glasses, to the office when she commits the slightest wrong. Then, the boys in the back will know you mean business.'

"I can still see myself that day: I was standing slightly behind him in my tweed jacket, striped tie, khaki pants, and loafers, peering through my clear-plastic-rimmed glasses at my new students. I was hardly older than the thirty of them sitting at their inkwell desks anchored to the floor. I listened but had no intention to follow his advice. I'd become a teacher because I loved kids. How could I send a 'good girl' to the office? I did have some trouble with the boys in the back, but talking with them before and after class helped us connect.

"Early on I learned to be patient whenever a student became disruptive. I would ask him to talk about his behavior and think about how to control it; self-regulation allows time to 'cool it' in stress situations. This process took time, but it was an important piece of my day. And I shifted from asking for external success, and instead, invited them to see the value of internal motivation—a long-term process for sure. Threatening them proved far less effective than offering invitations, which opened a door for them to want to learn.

"I saw the importance of recognizing empathic behavior. I made this a centerpiece of our conversations. In recent years, however, I've seen less empathy, which I think results from being on computers and excessive smartphone use. These young people feel freer to dis one another; cyberbully anonymously, something they would not do in person. And they're more separated. You see it as they arrive in the classroom; less chatting with each other and with me—and that they open their phones as soon as the bell rings."

Mr. Persons adjusted his sitting position and peered over his glasses, "As you can tell, I have sought ways to inculcate empathy. Recently, I showed *To Kill a Mockingbird*, which led to interesting discussions. Most understood the centrality of empathy in the film. The same was true when I showed *Billy Elliot*. And I've added Mark Haddon's, *The Curious Incident of the Dog in the Night-Time* to our reading list. These have stimulated my students' imagination by taking perspectives on others' feelings, thoughts, and views.

"I've asked students to practice recognizing others' feelings: anger, happiness, or sadness. The more aware they are of their own emotions, the better they're able to empathize. The more I demonstrate kindness, the better they come to understand it. You both must have noticed the absence of emotional literacy in many of your students. You'll need to find ways to instill it.

"And, I might add, I use pedagogies that require social interaction. I use triads for group work; they make for a quieter room, because only one person in a group speaks at a time. I wish I'd discovered this process years ago. I also use jigsaws, four corners, pair-shares, brief writings, one-on-one sharing, give-one-get-one, 10–2, chart-paper rotation, and others.[1] I would be glad to share these with you. Perhaps you could come and observe when I'm using one or more of these methods. These improve social skills, far better than teacher-talk—and require face-to-face interactions."

"Yes, I know of some of these approaches," said Harold, "but I did not realize how they could encourage empathy. I shall keep this in mind as I use them again."

Amanda added, "I'd like to learn more about them. I've only tried jigsaw but without much success."

"When I first heard about the concept random acts of kindness," said Mr. Persons, "it reminded me how important kindness is to social behavior.

I sometimes ask my kids at the beginning of class if they've seen an act of kindness, or even better, if they've done one. At first they were shy about this, but it's become a staple. Talking about kindness invites the mind to put it front and center—at least I think so. I also ask if anyone has stepped up to help another who's been bullied—a courageous act for a high schooler or for anyone. And some have enacted kindness by raising money for hurricane victims; others have helped renovate our community center.

"And I discovered another idea recently, one I hadn't thought about. One morning on the radio, I heard Dacher Keltner of the Greater Good Science Center at Berkeley speak about power of self-compassion.[2] No doubt you've seen kids who tend to be down on themselves, sometimes even self-loathing. For them to reach out with kindness, they first need to be kind to themselves. Keltner talks about the self-compassionate letter in which the person writes to himself from a third-person point of view. I like this idea and have had a few students write one. They seem to become less harsh on themselves. But it will take time.

"Take a look at their website. Their 'Keys to Well-Being' make sense to me: altruism, awe, compassion, social connection, diversity, empathy, forgiveness, gratitude, happiness, kindness, mindfulness, and optimism. The site is interactive. It bridges the gap between science and daily life, a good combination I think. You will enjoy spending time there.[3]

"And one more from Berkeley: 'Three Good Things.' It's an exercise that takes ten minutes at the end of the day. Write about three things that went well for you and offer reasons. It's important that you write them, then advocate, not simply think about them. I've begun to do it with my kids. Again, it's a positive, calming influence, something I'll take any day. On their website, they give specific instructions. Check it out for yourself.[4] And try it with your kids.

"When I started to focus more on emotional intelligence (EQ), I noticed as my students became self-aware and aware of the emotions of others, the calmer my room became. I began to see better work, more willingness to engage, and a greater sense of self-satisfaction. In 1995, Daniel Goleman published *Emotional Intelligence: Why It Can Matter More Than IQ*.[5] What surprised me was his articulation of what I'd come to understand. Goleman's summary of Peter Salovey's five domains of emotional intelligence hit home. Here are the five":

- *Knowing one's emotions.* Self-awareness—recognizing a feeling as it happens—is the keystone of emotional intelligence.
- *Managing emotions.* Handling feelings so they are appropriate is an ability that builds on self-awareness.

- *Motivating oneself.* Marshaling emotions in the service of a goal is essential for paying attention, for self-motivation, and for creativity.
- *Recognizing emotions in others.* Empathy, another ability that builds on emotional self-awareness, is the fundamental "people skill."
- *Handling relationships.* The art of relationships is, in large part, skill in managing the emotions in others.[6]

"I was pleased to learn that what I was evolving in my practice was verified by research. As I paid attention, I made adjustments to my practice and jettisoned some. Paying attention to my students' emotional behaviors led me to recognize their manifestation. You both will have to face unknown challenges, ones that may be even more difficult than distractions now caused by the smartphone culture. I suggest that you do not put your head in the sand or throw your hands up in despair. Deal with what's in front of you. Do your best. Ask for help. And include your kids when seeking solutions.

"The other point that we've not discussed," Mr. Persons emphasized, "has been the impact on smartphones on our kids—and on us. I struggle more to get their attention. I saw myself having to repeat more often. It was then I decided to have them put their phones in a basket when entering the room. It seemed to work, but I still sensed anxiety from many.

"But later I heard about Yondr from my friend Carolyn Hench, who learned about it from Lea Archer, her protégé. I wrote a grant and bought cases and the unlocking device. At first, many resisted putting their phone in the cases, but as weeks passed they became more attentive, not only to me but to each other, and my efforts with the emotional-intelligence side of my teaching improved."

"Thank you, Mr. Persons, for all your sharing," said Amanda. "I can see how you have the reputation for invoking strong relationships. I plan to read Goleman's book and make emotional intelligence more of a focus. And I can't wait to explore the Greater Good Science Center website."

"I agree with you, Amanda," said Harold. "I learned about Goleman's EQ in graduate school, but I will pay more attention to its benefits. I am grateful, Mr. Persons, for your account of how you came to see EQ as integral—and your discovery of the Berkeley site. And thanks for sharing about Yondr; I intend to look into it."

After getting second cups of coffee—Harold got a croissant—Mr. Persons suggested that they shift the conversation. "One of the backbones for me," he said in a quiet voice, "has been reflecting through the years on my process as a teacher and developing my philosophy. When Harold told me about you, Amanda, I thought that both of you would benefit from my stance. Examining myself within a greater context has provided a perspective on who I am, what I care about, and in finding meaning in what I do every day. I happen to have a selected version in my briefcase, which we can discuss." He handed them a copy:

- Teaching is an enormously complex activity—and has the potential to be deeply satisfying. This has been my mantra. Teachers may embrace it or resist. As Ziggy exclaims, "You can complain because roses have thorns, or you can rejoice because thorns have roses."
- Teaching to be deeply satisfying requires a willingness to be transformed.
- It happens where invitations abound, where questions prevail, where unknowns thrive.
- Honest teaching is joyous. Nothing rivals the magic of being in communion with children and manifesting the gifts that each of them holds dear. Being there, listening, observing, describing, waiting, and attending without judgment is at the heart of this joy.
- Good teaching holds high expectations for all. No child arrives with a fixed intelligence, fixed emotional capabilities, or a fixed self-concept. They tend to learn as little or as much as teachers expect. Implementing a growth mind-set and setting and communicating high expectations promotes greater academic performance and personal satisfaction.
- Know yourself. Be true to your character.
- Teach for lifelong learning. Model your instruction, dwell on the unexpected, and look for surprises. Keep the door open.
- Design curricula that focuses on understanding and devises ways students can demonstrate it.
- Teachers do important work. You may be the last best hope for children.
- Resolve to give up worksheets, those fill-in pieces of paper. I heard a first grader say, "We don't learn in this class. We do worksheets." That's enough reason to ban them.
- Avoid freeze-dried lessons, instantly usable formats that diminish potential. As John Dewy said, "The road of the new education is not an easier one to follow than the old road but a more strenuous and difficult one."[7]
- Stay on the edge. Whatever your curriculum, see it as your own. Stretch your imagination to stretch their imaginations.
- Pay attention. To everything. To each student. To their parents. To your colleagues. To the administration. To the culture of your school. Be in it, of it—and outside of it when you must.
- Get out of yourself. See your children for who they are, each unique, each needing you to know that. Let them know you know them, each one of them.

"That's quite a list," said Harold. "I like your comprehensive take, but I'll need time to digest it. It's far beyond what I thought about teaching when I was in graduate school. I intend to look closer at my practice."

Amanda added, "I've never thought about the importance of honing my own philosophy. I came into the profession thinking that I needed to be like my teachers, but I've found it difficult replicating them. For one, my kids are nothing like I was at their age. For another, I see myself becoming different. Reading this list opens the door for me to articulate who I am and my beliefs—and to celebrate them!"

"Ditto," said Harold. "I connect with your first statement about the complexity of our vocation. Teachers face daily challenges often unforeseen. Unlike doctors who have one patient at a time, we deal with twenty-five or more 'patients' several times a day. Some researchers have said the we are second to air-traffic controllers in the amount of decisions we make. Some days I can hardly keep up, but know I must, and I wouldn't miss this complexity for anything. It keeps me on my toes. No day is like another."

"I feel the same way," said Amanda. "I see myself establishing a path of lifelong learning. It seems silly to jump small hurdles without seeing the long road ahead. Mr. Persons, you remind me of teaching for understanding, something my graduate school teachers stressed."

"Teaching for understanding is one of my favorite concepts," said Mr. Persons. "Can I ask what you two think in this time of intense outside expectations and testing about the idea of putting yourself on the edge of your curriculum, about making it your own?"

After a pause, Harold replied, "You seem to be implying that you want us to teach our own way. You'd like to hear our students in the hallway say, 'Do you know what just happened in Mr. Coughlin's class?' I bet you'd like to hear that coming out of every classroom."

"One of the reasons I came to this school was to experience that," said Amanda. "I want the freedom and support to reach kids my way, not the expected ways. In department meetings at my former school, the mind-set of 'staying on the same page' dominated. I hated it, as each of my classes needed different nurturing to get through the material. But being new, I found it difficult to challenge this system. It made no sense."

"And I like your last two premises, Mr. Persons," said Harold. "'Pay attention'; what could be more important than to see what's in front of me! Thanks for pointing this out. And 'Get out of yourself' will be a challenge. Having the confidence to step away from my personal zone and into others' space is not easy. I've done it sometimes; other times I hesitate. Your stating this principle encourages me."

With that comment, Mr. Persons suggested they call it a day. It had been well over two and a half hours. "I'd like to leave you with a quotation from Loren Eiseley that has been important to me. I carry it in my wallet":

> It is here, amid a chaos of complexities, that the teacher, frequently with blindness, with uncertainties of his own, must fight with circumstance for the developing mind—perhaps even for the very survival of the child . . . the teacher is fighting for an oncoming future, for something that has not emerged, which may, in fact, never emerge . . . the teacher is a sculptor of the intangible future.[8]

"'A sculptor of the intangible future,'" said Harold. We *are* in a serious profession. I'll take that challenge. May I have a copy of that quotation?" Amanda asked for one as well.

NOTES

1. You can find these and other ideas in my other two books with Rowman & Littlefield: *Teaching That Matters: Engaging Minds, Improving Schools* (2014) and *Exciting Classrooms: Practical Information to Ensure Student Success* (2015).

2. Dacher Keltner, "Episode 2: Quieting Your Inner Critic," podcast The Science of Happiness, https://greatergood.berkeley.edu/podcasts/item/quieting_your_inner_critic.

3. https://greatergood.berkeley.edu.

4. Go to ggia.berkeley.edu and click "Remember Three Good Things."

5. Daniel Goleman, *Emotional Intelligence: Why It Can Matter More Than IQ* (New York: Bantam, 1995).

6. Ibid., 43.

7. John Dewey, *Experience and Education* (New York: Touchstone, 1938), 90.

8. Loren Eiseley, *The Night Country: Reflections of a Bone-Hunting Man* (New York: Charles Scribner's Sons, 1971), 200.

Chapter 13

To Google or Not to Google

Don Jorgensen, Amy Watson, Gordon Mason, and Bonnie Canton

Maybe if there were two monks . . .

Don Jorgensen retired at the turn of the century. He'd taught a range of subjects in middle and high school, including social studies, language arts, math, and drama—clearly a versatile teacher. He was known for lessons that prodded and teased. For the past five years, before the opening of school, the principal invited Don to talk with new teachers. After the morning induction meeting, Mr. Jorgensen met with Amy Watson, Gordon Mason, and Bonnie Canton in the library.

Amy, hired to teach middle school language arts, arrived first. She was wearing glasses hanging on a gold chain in front of her red blouse, a long black skirt, and was tall and slender, with blonde hair swept back and a big smile on her face. She'd heard about Mr. Jorgensen's reputation. Gordon, new to the high school math department, came after her. Energetic, wearing khakis and a blue open-collar shirt, he was humming and twirling his fingers, his eyebrows up, his hair disheveled.

Behind him came Bonnie, a science teacher in the middle school. She was wearing her white lab coat, having just set up her lab. Demure but focused, a warm smile beneath her tortoiseshell glasses, she had close-cropped light brown hair. They sat in the three chairs Mr. Jorgensen had set out.

Mr. Jorgensen was pleased to meet them as he observed their alert attitudes and obvious interest. He always looked for passion in teachers. After hearing Amy, Gordon, and Bonnie explain how they became teachers—they all saw it as a calling—he opened the meeting with a surprise. He took a piece of paper out of a folder and read it aloud:

104   Chapter 13

> One morning, exactly at sunrise, a Buddhist monk began to climb a tall mountain. The narrow path, no more than a foot or two wide, spiraled around the mountain to a glittering temple at the summit.
>   The monk ascended the path at varying rates of speed, stopping many times along the way to rest and to eat the dried fruit he carried. He reached the temple shortly before sunset. After several days of fasting and meditation, he began his journey back along the same path, starting at sunrise and again walking at variable speeds, taking many pauses along the way. His average speed descending was, of course, greater than his average climbing speed.
>   Prove there is a single spot along the path the monk will occupy on both trips at precisely the same time of day.[1]

Amy asked him to read it a second time. "This is a strange problem," she said. "I don't see how the monk could be at the same place at the same time on both days." Gordon and Bonnie slowly nodded. The problem was unlike any they'd ever heard.

Mr. Jorgensen supplied background as to why he shared this problem. "While I was working in a private middle school, the head called me into his office to tell me I would be teaching ancient history instead of American history. It was a radical change, one I did not anticipate. It would be challenging to make the course rich and deep after years of teaching American history. After much careful planning, I wanted to find an opening to set the tone for investigating the wisdom of the ancients—my intended focus.

"I came across this problem from a friend. He challenged me to solve it. That night I sat at my desk, fiddled with my pencil on graph paper. A half-hour later, much to my surprise, I solved it. I thought it would be good to present it to my eighth graders. I gave it to them on the first day of ancient history.

"You can imagine their reactions, much like yours, Amy":

> "It's not possible, Mr. Jorgensen, for the monk to be in one place at two different times. It's just not possible!"
>   "If the monk arrives earlier at the bottom of the trail he can't be at the same spot on the trail on both days."
>   "Staying several days at the top complicates the problem. Maybe if he left the next morning, he'd have a better chance to arrive at the same spot."

"However, a few students started to break the problem down. One wondered how fasting and meditation had anything to do with the solution and another brought up the possibility that there was another monk.

"My students left perplexed and with no homework assignment. They would surely seek help from their parents at the dinner table—remember those days?—and come in the next morning with solutions, which several did. By the end of the period, most were able to visualize the monk at the same place on the path at the same time on both days.

"Still some left shaking their heads. I told them—and wanted them to tell their parents—that in this class we will seek our own answers, not look for them in a textbook or get them from authorities. We will probe ideas, ask questions, challenge thinking—theirs and mine. We'll not simply take in stuff from other sources but think and reach our own conclusions.

"And my decision to use the monk problem did not come out of nowhere. While I was in college—not an honors student by any means—I developed a tendency to probe issues, to question stuff, to be a philosopher if you will. Why, I don't know.

"It first manifested at my waiters' table in my dorm. Each of the five of us had his role, from Tom's specializing in double-talk to Ron's keeping order—and I was the philosopher: 'Oh no, here goes Don again. He's on a roll!' Ron would say. He'd reach back with his right hand to the wall to light up the imagined philosophy machine. The others rolled their eyes.

"So, Amy, Bonnie, and Gordon, would you be willing to use this problem in your classes? Do you think it would work today?" They barely heard Mr. Jorgensen, because they were wrestling to find the solution. Mr. Jorgensen sat back. For the next ten minutes they turned the problem over and over but got nowhere. The notion of visualizing two monks on the trail elicited some clarity. Suddenly, Gordon reached to pull out his iPhone from his pocket.

"Stop, Gordon," said Mr. Jorgensen. "Please don't do that."

Gordon looked perplexed.

"Don't be confused, let me explain. Years after I used the monk-on-the-mountain problem, the Internet arrived, soon followed by Google.

"I googled monk-on-the-mountain and, voila, there were numerous explanations waiting for my click. Had Google existed when I offered the problem, my students and I wouldn't have had conversations, and up until this moment, we would not have had ours."

"But why not google?" Gordon asked. Amy and Bonnie shook their heads in agreement.

"Think back, all of you, to the beginning of our meeting. Had I given you the problem and suggested that you google, what would we have talked about? What thinking would you have done? What speculations would you have made? What would you have discovered?

"I'm going to be up-front with you. By the way, call me Mr. J; I prefer that. I see kids searching Google before thinking, speculating, pondering. And Siri leads them to answers; simply ask and she'll provide. Frankly, I think this is a tragedy. Information derived from phones does not equal information assumed by the brain. Without learning, without absorbing knowledge, people may not develop their long-term memories, necessary for thinking through a problem. Not developing discernment means less access to the world. Without learning, there is more room to accept lies and half-truths—and sound-bites prevail.

"And I've noticed, these kids do not have language at the level we saw before Google. Language usage has been essential in human evolution. To lose its depth will relegate people to absorb sound-bites and half-truths, become receptacles of words rather than creators. And Google Home and Amazon's Echo and Alexa—think of the dependency, another excuse not to use your mind! Perhaps I'm extreme. What do you think, Bonnie?"

Bonnie, who'd been quiet, raised her eyebrows. "I've never thought about it this way. I admit, I'm enjoying the struggle to solve the monk problem. I don't want someone—like Google—to tell me the solution. I've been stripping away its nonessentials: 'the narrow path,' 'glittering temple,' 'eat dried fruit he carried,' 'after several days of fasting and meditating,' 'waking at variable speeds,' 'taking pauses along the way.'"

For the budding science teacher, Mr. J thought, the problem was becoming clearer.

"But I wonder," said Amy returning to Mr. J's point, "how can we stop the onslaught of Siri, Echo, or Google Home? They are so tempting, addictive, and, I think, demeaning. Ads, such as 'ask the smart-speaker,' implies it knows more than you do. Why make an effort to investigate if you only need to ask?

"And like Google Maps, which I love, once you rely on GPS, you become less able to read printed maps. It's like losing handwriting skills after word processing. The world is changing—and it's happening fast. Can we really slow down this digital-audio invasion? It seems that everywhere we turn there is a digital device waiting for us. And more and more apps available to work for us! Insisting we pay attention."

"You know," Gordon said quizzically, "Mr. J, since you told me to put my phone in my pocket, you're encouraging me to think about the role of Google in my life. Recently a friend said that being on our phones could be compared to a man plowing his field where he's free to think. The man's alone—except with his plow horse—having no contact with anyone except his wife at lunch, then dinner, and possibly the evening unless he goes directly to bed. So, my friend asked me, what's the difference for the person on the phone?

"I answered, the man plowing his field knows he's alone. However, the person on his phone thinks he's not alone. That's the fallacy. He's in contact, but he's not *with* anyone. Neither he nor his contacts connect except through photos—and on Snapchat those dissolve—or through an exchange of texts. That's how I see it and why I'm convinced that I need to have my kids be with one another in my classroom.

"My friend also argued," Gordon pressed, "that the man plowing his field is thinking, and the man on his phone for hours on end is also a thinker. Again, I disagreed. The man in the field is not distracted while thinking; in fact, he's focused on his work; he's in his mind. While the man on the phone sends and receives information, or he looks for more information spending little time—even a few seconds if that—on what he finds. Unless he comes away from his phone, he is not thinking."

"Interesting ideas, Gordon," said Mr. J. "I've been digging into this issue. There are so many facets to consider. We know that phones are alluring, so much so that teens text 3,300 times—girls 4,000—per month, or every six minutes while awake. The same holds true for adults.

"People stay on a webpage for an average of ten seconds, no matter the content. Phones grab us to pay attention, except we don't really pay attention because in seconds we move on to the next thing. Paying attention happens when we cut away from searching for information and take time to assess what's important. Unless we get off the phone merry-go-round, we'll allow Google and Facebook to decide for us—and that would be a tragedy.

"Nicholas Carr said it best, a quote I carry with me":

> If we sacrifice that fundamental quality of our mind, the ability to determine for ourselves what we are going to think about and how much time we spend thinking about it, then for all the gains of the Internet has giving us will be sacrificing the most important thing that governs the depth of our thought.[2]

"So, the three of you appear to want your students to step away from seeking and relaying information and be together. Yet, sometimes I think the trend to rely on digital devices may become the norm. I'd like to think, however, that humans will still enjoy—and insist—on spending time together, at least I hope so."

"Curious," said Bonnie. "I agree with you, Mr. J, but when I watch my teens, they're making friends through their phones. It's their means to be together. It's been my means, too, not entirely but certainly more recently. My kids rely on them as the generation before me relied on passing notes in school and getting phone calls at home or on our answering machines.

"While I think that solely relying on phones is fraught with complications, I have to acknowledge their presence." Bonnie took a deep breath. "I don't think we should put our heads in the sand and simply have them put away their phones. That puts us in an adversarial position. Instead, we should show that we understand their relationship with the phone and help them navigate their way with and without them.

"But we only have them for one period a day. The rest of the time they are with other teachers who may not agree with our point of view. Still, we should take time to teach them to use their phones well. For instance, I'm going to plan a unit where we take them out in class and surf the Internet. I want them to learn to distinguish good sites from bad ones—and develop a nose for knowing the difference. I'm not sure how this will work, but I'll do my best. As for confronting the incessant texting, I don't know what to do."

Amy, who'd been listening carefully, said, "I think we need to go further. Being sensible in our classrooms is one thing but not enough. My biggest concern about the phone is its power to facilitate cyberbullying. We know this is a huge issue in our school, in all schools. I think we need to meet with Principal Davenport and set up a program that teaches students how to use their phones responsibly. Otherwise, the lowest common denominator will prevail and cyberbullying will be unchecked. We all need to be on the same page. We can't pretend it's not happening. We'll need outside help to make a successful program."

And Bonnie added, "We may be pessimistic about today's kids. However, I'd like to think—perhaps I'm overly optimistic—that maybe, just maybe, they will surprise us. I can't imagine they'll not find their way out of the digital swirl and discover depths of self waiting for them. Think of the little ones on iPads and their creativity. Adults sometimes speak about adolescents as if they do not believe in them. I'm betting that we can help them come to know each other, listen to each other, to us, and feel the joy of the personal without intermediary devices.

"In fact, I've taken time to listen to my students. Not only about what they say about what we're doing in class but listening to them, about who they are, and what they care about. I want them to know that I am here for them. I am 'wonderfully curious'[3] about who they are and how they feel about school and their community. I want to get behind behaviors I don't understand—excessive app focus for example—to a place where they know I care about them. I'll be a better teacher, and they'll be better students—at least I'm banking on it."

"I love this idea, Bonnie," said Amy. "You have opened a door I should have seen, one that lets students know we will listen to them, their concerns, their joys, their lives. We need to let go of any obsession we may have about overuse of the smartphone. After all, we use them, far more than our parents. If we appear to judge them because we think they are too close to their devices, they will judge us and keep us at bay, feign courtesy, and/or actively resist. They need to know we are here for them—and we need to be the adult in the room."

"Whoa, I have another idea," said Bonnie. "Why haven't I thought about this before? Given our conversation about smartphones—good and bad—I am thinking of beginning a class by holding up my smartphone and asking this: 'What is it that I *can't* get from this?' And just hold it up. I imagine some quiet at first, but I'm sure someone will begin the conversation. It could prove enlightening."

"This has been quite the conversation," said Mr. J. "You three impress me with your enthusiasm and willingness to deal head-on with your students. To teach students to understand that their relentless passing on of information is one thing, but stepping away from that process and thinking deeply about what's important is essential: to gain knowledge, to be reflective, creative, and think critically, these are the highest aspects of human thinking. You could not give your students a better gift. And your idea to hold up the phone and ask, 'What is it that I can't get from this?' should be revealing. I hope you'll share what you find out. I plan to try this myself.

"All of you—Gordon, Amy, and Bonnie—have influence on how your students act inside the swirl of digital media. You are the deciders. Begin by committing to a classroom grounded in real information. Don't allow soundbites. Be sure at times that all smartphones are out of pocket in a cubby or basket—and turned off. Have them sit face to face with you, with each other. Help them look into each other's eyes when they speak. Have them paraphrase what someone else has said. Show them empathy. Have them learn the art of conversation.

"And—here's a clincher—I want to share what I learned recently from a friend who has worked in IT for over thirty years. He told me that he's more than twice as old as his coworkers; they're all in their twenties and thirties. At lunch, they bring their phones. 'They appear to multitask comfortably (actually, serial-task),' he told me, 'shifting from their phones into the conversation and out again. They have no problem with it. And neither do I.'

"My friend's observation has me thinking that maybe your kids will sort out living with their phones in ways we can't imagine. I'd like to think my friend's observation offers a clue, but I still think we need to nurture conversation skills.

"And one more point: Listen to these warnings from George Soros, which he gave at Davos. I've brought a copy of the article for each of you; I'll read an excerpt and add my comments":

> Social Media companies are inducing people to give up their autonomy. . . . It takes a real effort to assert and defend what John Stuart Mill called "the freedom of mind." There is a possibility that, once lost, people who grow up in the digital age will have difficulty in regaining it. This may have far-reaching political consequences. People without the freedom of mind can be easily manipulated.[4]

And Soros, who is in his late eighties, takes it far beyond implications for the classroom. The potential for the great IT giants Facebook and Google's corporate surveillance combined with state-sponsored surveillance could result, he said, in a "web of totalitarian control the likes of which not even Aldous Huxley or George Orwell could have imagined."[5]

"Perhaps keeping that possible end in view in mind will alert you to your task."

Mr. J suggested they take a break, get another coffee or tea and perhaps a pastry. He wanted to share another idea before they broke up, one different but nonetheless important. After they settled back down, he took out Margaret Wheatley's six principles for valuing conversations and gave each a copy:

> We acknowledge one another as equals.
> We try to stay curious about each other.
> We recognize that we need each other's help to become better listeners.
> We slow down so we have time to think and reflect.
> We remember that conversation is the natural way we humans think together.
> We expect it to be messy at times.[6]

"*Acknowledge* others as equals," Mr. J said, "Allow each person to be heard; no one is more important. *Stay curious*, listen, pay attention, and be patient. Become *better listeners*, note body language, tone, and innuendo. *Slow down* to think and allow time for ideas to be absorbed. *Conversation* is natural, where texting, Snapchat, Instagram, and other apps isolate. Make your classroom a space outside this skipping-stones-across-the pond-information sharing, a space for pondering. And yes, recognize that conversation is *messy*—and why shouldn't it be?"

Gordon Mason was taken by Wheatley's principles. He intended to listen to his digital kids, to learn about their life practices. They were so different from him when he was an adolescent. "I like the first principle, 'acknowledge one another as equals'; it will let my kids know that we are in this adventure together, and it won't be good if I impose my ideas. My classroom will be an invitation to learn, not a regurgitation factory."

Amy Watson came into teaching thinking she would bring knowledge and skills, but Gordon led her to think of another perspective: to build respect. Showing respect would tell her students that she would be alongside them: "I don't want to be seen as the one-who-knows and delivers but as one who listens and brings what I've learned into the conversation."

Bonnie Canton brought up children's increasing isolation. She knew of families who would text one another from within the home. Upstairs, a teenager would text Mom to bring up a grilled cheese with mustard for dinner—and Mom would oblige. Some parents chose to argue through texting from different rooms; it was less emotional, and the kids would not have to hear them arguing. "Sherry Turkle has written about this.[7] And commentaries have appeared in newspapers."[8]

Mr. J was impressed with his three new protégés. "It has been an honor to have been with all of you, to hear your intelligent comments, and to know that three classrooms will have dynamic new teachers. As for the monk-on-the-mountain problem, I'll leave it to you to ponder. I hope you do not submit to the temptation to google it. Let your minds do their thing. You'll be better for it. You will know when you have the answer!

"As for our conversation about smartphones, I am coming away with lots of wisdom. I thank you for that. We need to gain the attention of our students, a more challenging task than I ever remember. I'm confident that you will find success.

"And I hope you will think about what you bring into your classrooms, what experiences have fed into your becoming the teacher you are. Knowing yourself will help you become a better teacher. Take time to reflect on who you are and how you got there.

"Let's agree to meet at the end of September. You will have been in the thick of things for another month and should have lots to talk about. And I will bring in another idea or two. Thanks for coming. See you then."

NOTES

1. Arthur Koestler, *The Act of Creation* (London: Hutchinson, 1964), 183–84. Koestler refers to the June 1961 issue of *Scientific American* as his source and that the problem originated from the psychologist Carl Duncker.

2. Nicholas Carr, "What the Internet Is Doing to Our Brains," Moses Znaimer's Ideacity 2015 Conference, September 28, 2015.

3. Rob Fried used this phrase in sharing the idea that teachers should begin the year letting students know that they are, in fact, "wonderfully curious" about their lives.

4. John Cassidy, "How George Soros Upstaged Donald Trump at Davos," *The New Yorker*, January 25, 2018.

5. Ibid.

6. Margaret Wheatley, *Turning to One Another: Simple Conversations to Restore Hope to the Future* (San Francisco: Berrett-Koehler, 2002), 29.

7. Turkle, *Reclaiming Conversation*, 105.

8. Beth Teitell, "The Texts Are Coming from Inside the House," *Boston Globe*, September 21, 2017.

Chapter 14

Stay Grounded in Reality

Don Jorgensen, Amy Watson, Gordon Mason, and Bonnie Canton

Belief has its place.

Before they knew it, Amy Watson, Gordon Mason, and Bonnie Canton were back in the library with Mr. J. They had many stories to share but wanted to allot most of the time for him. They'd already hashed out their first weeks together. They valued keeping in close contact to avoid the perils of the isolated classroom. They each had a mentor who helped them learn the ropes, but they liked staying close and met frequently after school.

Amy brought up that she has invoked a listening attitude in her classroom. At first, she wasn't sure how to balance listening with giving the lesson, but the more she mixed the two, the better her lessons became; and the better her listening. Gordon restrained himself from googling the monk-on-the-mountain, but he found it a struggle to avoid clicking for the solution. Bonnie added that she and Gordon discussed the problem and thought they have the answer; perhaps later, they could talk about it. Bonnie also reported that she'd begun to apply Wheatley's six principles for discussions in her science classes and liked how well they worked.

The three were excited. Their classrooms were becoming more engaging. They were feeling that their rooms may be the last vestige of hope where students could discover the joy of being together without intermediary devices.

Mr. J, hearing these comments, smiled and leaned forward in his chair. "Today, I want to bring up an issue dear to my heart. We live in a culture where nearly half the people do not believe in evolution, and where it is much higher in evangelical groups. They believe the earth is only 6,000–10,000 years old. They're suspect of science. In response to these beliefs, some schools deal with this 'controversy' by placing creationism alongside evolution, a false equivalence.

"I've been a person grounded in reality. I've aimed for truth, to what is supported by evidence, not purported as beliefs. Belief has its place. We all need it at some points in our lives, but it has no place in the classroom. Unsupported beliefs imperil thinking just as sound-bites shortchange it. From my earliest days, I've made seeking the truth my mantra.

"So, when it came to ancient history, as I shared with you last time, I was concerned how to make the course a search for truth. I thought about the traditional view for the course, which begins with the late hunter-gatherers and the first civilizations (i.e., the human arrival on the earth's stage 200,000 years ago).

"But what about the billions of years before? One could argue that this is not part of ancient history, as scholars claim history should be based on the written word. I thought differently. How could we understand our presence on earth without connecting with how we got here? From that moment in my thinking, I resolved to begin my course with the Big Bang—or the Big Bloom as I later understood it."

Bonnie Canton's eyebrows shot up. "You began ancient history with the Big Bang? How could you possibly do that? No textbook that I've seen covers that. Only recently have we known that the universe is 13.7 billion years old. It's one of my favorite topics. I hope, Mr. J, you will show me ways to introduce it." Amy and Gordon were fascinated as well and did not know much about it but were ready to listen.

Mr. J recounted that he taught the universe story in the late 1990s. He'd become fascinated ten years before when he discovered Carl Sagan's *Cosmos*.[1] His opening words, some of which he put to memory:

> The Cosmos is all that is or ever was or ever will be. . . . We wish to pursue the truth no matter where it leads, but to find the truth we need imagination and skepticism both. . . . The Cosmos is within us. We are made of star stuff. We are a way for the Cosmos to know itself.

From that moment Mr. J understood his search for truth would be on the right path. It would be on a cosmic scale. How could he possibly not keep this perspective active in his life, in his classroom? According to Sagan, the planet was precious and in peril. Yet, Mr. J said to his three protégés with a heavy heart, "We've ignored Sagan's warnings. We are in deeper peril today with the deleterious effects of climate change. Perhaps when schools take his *Cosmos* perspective into their curriculum, children will understand this."

Amy, Gordon, and Bonnie saw Mr. J almost in tears. He wiped his eyes as he began to tell how he infused this perspective. "I was determined," he began, "not to *tell* the universe story to my students. No matter how well I might've told it, my telling would have diminished chances for them to internalize Sagan's perspective. I considered showing excerpts of the *Cosmos* series, but I didn't. Today, I would reconsider and perhaps show five-to-ten-minute bites of Brian Swimme's *Canticle to the Cosmos*.[2] And I would give thought to having my students read Swimme and Mary Evelyn Tucker's *Journey of the Universe*[3] and watch the accompanying film.

"If you are to be grounded in reality, you need to do it every day. You need to live inside your material with your students. If, for example, you choose to share information via text or images to individual smartphones or tablets, you will have no opportunity to interact, to question, assess, and ponder. You communicate but without the potential for ah-ha's when face to face. Such ah-ha's sets imagination and thinking to new territory. I wouldn't miss that!"

Bonnie liked the idea of showing five-to-ten-minute bites from Sagan's episodes (or Swimme's Canticles) to enrich her science curriculum. Mr. J agreed with her decision. He explained that some of his colleagues often showed full-length films, which he felt created a passive audience, as kids have been saturated with videos. "Using clips effectively, Bonnie, is a smart idea. You create hunger, a hunger to speak to one another, to listen, to know, understand, and act."

Gordon turned to Mr. J and asked, "How did you infuse curiosity about the universe's billions of years? That seems like an esoteric topic."

"As I look back on those days, I think one factor was my enthusiasm. I knew I couldn't have been presenting something further from their lives. Having conversations with a colleague, I became excited about new thinking about the Big Bang. He led me to Brian Swimme and Thomas Berry's *The Universe Story*,[4] a new perspective on the origin of universe and earth.

"Second, I became passionate about doing the course. There's something exciting about being the first and the only teacher doing something. I liked being out on a limb, to take a new adventure and to bring my eighth graders along. It energized my teaching, something you'll understand when you do it. And as we discussed, I set a tone for my ancient history course with the monk-on-the-mountain problem. From there we pondered multiple perspectives of the Big Bang.

"The first reading in the course—and the most provocative—addressed the concept that the visual universe is made up of atoms, which include humans. Given the fact that atoms are 99 percent emptiness, each one of us are 99 percent empty! Imagine my students' bewilderment. They even poked themselves trying to understand. While hard to fathom, most came to understand this concept even if they could not 'see' it. By now they knew they were in for a wild ride!

"From there, I gave a one-page handout, 'The Web of Life,' that pointed out that billions of years of life arose in the universe that not only reproduced and but also represent itself; the emergence of the universe could not be random. From here, conversations in each class erupted. I vividly remember comments." Mr. J reached into his vest pocket:

"Until I came in to this class, I believed that the universe was always here. I had no idea that it began 13.7 billion years ago. I have difficulty imagining that."

"I can imagine that what's happened in the universe has not been random, nor has it been done by God. I think there's something in the mix, call it consciousness perhaps, which has worked to get us here."

"There's no way that our being here is an accident. And I agree God did not do it."

"I know that God put us here, I'm sure of that. There's no way that universe has evolved over billions of years. The earth is only 10,000 years old."

"This last comment stays etched in my mind. It awakened me to my mission not to convey to the choir but to seek the truth even when uncomfortable. But when 'truths' contradicted, I treaded a gentle road. For the rest of the six weeks, I was aware of this girl's views and listened to her concerns. The truth, I hope, that emerged was the right of each person to hold onto her truth. Could I have taught the universe story in an evangelical school? Perhaps I wouldn't have chosen to—nor would I have been allowed."

Amy brought up the current conversations around being politically correct. "I wonder if this mind-set gets in the way of becoming grounded in reality. Because we do not want to offend anyone, we may offend everyone. What I'm getting at, trying to stay politically correct on issues no one understands any part of. No one gets to feel anything. Instead, the issue may become a dry set of words, impossible to engage in dialogue, to flesh out different sides."

Gordon sat up and asked, "Are we to let the onslaught of digital information run past without paying attention to it? I've noticed how much my kids seem to know: about TV shows, actors, movies, the news, music, music videos, video games. They are replete with information. Yet, they can't seem to articulate meanings. I ask a question, sometimes get an answer but not much thought about the answer. It seems to me the universe story, as you are telling us, could encourage students to seek meaning. I'm thinking that may be our most essential job."

Mr. J was impressed with his protégés' insights and feeling good about their place in his former school. He was fortunate in his time that the concept of politically correct was in the future. He never hesitated to speak the truth as he understood it. Sometimes parents or colleagues would challenge him. He would listen but did not back down unless he was proved wrong.

Mr. J returned to Carl Sagan, the next piece in his universe unit. "I passed out Sagan's insightful Cosmic Calendar, which showed humans arriving on earth on December 31 at 10:30 p.m. Ancient history—as defined in textbooks—began just before the invention of agriculture at 11:59:20—forty seconds before today! I pointed out that our exploration of the universe via Sagan's calendar had covered eleven months, thirty days, and nearly twenty-four hours. And—what blew us away—civilized life on the planet equaled a coat of paint on the World Trade Center.

"Edwin Hubble's insights came next. In 1919, through his telescope, Hubble discovered that galaxies were all moving away from one another. Invoking the raisin bread metaphor, I invited my students to imagine sitting on one of the raisins and seeing others on raisins receding from them—and those on their raisins were seeing the same way. Space was expanding, and the earth is where it is—the center of the universe! Adolescents liked that thinking! Einstein, however, did not believe that galaxies were moving away from each other until he looked through Hubble's telescope."

To help tie things together, Mr. J shared an old joke (he gave them a copy):

> There's an old joke about a King who goes to a Wiseperson and asks how is it that the Earth doesn't fall down. The Wiseperson replies, "The Earth is resting on a lion." "On what, then, is the lion resting?" "The lion is resting on an elephant." "On what is the elephant resting?" "The elephant is resting on a turtle." "On what is the . . . ?" "You can stop right there, Your Majesty. It's turtles all the way down."[5]

Gordon sat up and with a smile said, "Had I been a student in your class, Mr. J, my mind would have been introduced to a whole new way of perceiving my place on the planet. 'Turtles all the way down' seals it. We are all connected from the very beginning and now with one another. I shall keep this mind-set in my practice."

Amy nodded in agreement. Bonnie indicated, too, that she was planning to include the universe story as part of her science curriculum. She'd already reviewed early episodes from Sagan's *Cosmos* and read the first three chapters of Swimme and Berry's *The Universe Story*. She also intended to read Swimme and Tucker's *Journey of the Universe*.

Mr. J shared two more perspectives. The first was Swimme and Berry's insight on simplifying knowledge. He saw it as a caution against testing as the determining factor for assessing achievement. He handed Amy, Gordon, and Bonnie a copy.

> For knowledge of understanding to be reduced to one-dimensionality—as with certain scientific tendencies to reduce all knowledge to the quantitative mode—would be similar to reducing a whole symphony to a single note. An integral

relationship with the universe's differentiated energy constellations requires a multivalent understanding that includes the full spectrum of modes of knowing.[6]

"'Reducing a whole symphony to a single note.' Wow!" said Bonnie. "A vivid metaphor. I'm going to make sure that my science students understand the power of metaphors and become comfortable with them."

"The same for me in language arts," said Amy. "Seeking metaphors and finding the diverse interpretations of poems, stories, plays will be my centerpiece."

"And for math," said Gordon, "I want to move away for the one-correct-answer-syndrome and stress the beauty of seeking alternative solutions to problems."

"Great ideas, you guys," said Mr. J. His second perspective also came from Swimme and Berry, who offered a framework for describing characteristics of all species in the universe. He handed each of them a card.

> *Differentiation, Communion,* and *Autopoiesis* framework, a way of understanding my students: each as complex and *different*; each with the capacity, to connect and *communicate*; and each capable of *autopoiesis*: self-generating as discoverer, creator, inventor, designer.[7]

"When I was in school, most of my classes were one-note: teachers delivering rather than provoking, telling rather than engaging. And I've seen colleagues perpetuating this mode. I sense that you all will make your classrooms symphonies, each student an instrument, each expression a note.

"And another point"—Mr. J was on a roll—"I showed Ron Fricke's breathtaking film *Baraka*,[8] shot in twenty-five countries and six continents, which had taken thirty months to complete. After the film, one girl wrote":

> When I think of the two views of the universe—and think about living in the expanded one—I think of a museum exhibit. The information we uncovered about our universe is like the brochure you get. Not many people get to experience this exhibit. I feel privileged to experience it. I am one of the select few.

Bonnie had seen *Baraka* a couple of times. It still spoke to her. She offered to show it to Amy and Gordon at her home. Mr. J then told them how he brought his universe story to a close, not with a test but by having students write their own universe stories. He'd given spot quizzes along the way but wanted to hear their thinking rather than responses to his questions. He was more than surprised with the results and kept copies of several of them. He offered to let Amy, Gordon, and Bonnie read them.

They ended their meeting and agreed to reconvene later in the term.

The next weekend the three young teachers met at Bonnie's to see *Baraka*; Mr. J was not able to come. After the film, which they agreed was profound, they sat around Bonnie's dining room table to discuss their times with Mr. J.

"I am so grateful," said Amy, "to know Mr. J. He's been a great role model for the path we are choosing. I can barely take it all in. I will need time to absorb his thinking and transfer his ideas into my twenty-first-century classroom. I will do my best."

"Me too," said Gordon. "I remember Mr. J's reaction when I took out my phone to google the monk-on-the-mountain problem. He put me off at first, but he convinced me to provoke thinking without phones, even having to become frustrated in the process. My students will have to wrestle with information, as I've had to with the monk problem. This process will improve their long-term memories. In an 1892 lecture, William James said, 'The art of remembering is the art of thinking.' I want my kids to have memories filled with knowledge so they can process their thinking."

Bonnie interjected, "I've invoked Wheatley's six principles as an integral part of my classroom. They've convinced me to provoke face-to-face thinking. And the messy part, her sixth principle, has allowed for some exciting conversations."

Amy added, "I've picked up on Wheatley's list, too. And I've challenged my impulsive kids to hold their thoughts, to listen to what others are saying, pause and reconsider what they might say and only then raise their hand. This process has taken a lot of time, but they're getting better. Sometimes, to encourage listening, I ask a student to paraphrase what he heard from another before he offers his response."

"More of my kids are speaking thoughtfully," Amy continued. "They are learning to take in other opinions and points of view without judging or condemning them. And I'm going to incorporate tablets. I intend to ask them to write down their thinking and with Google Drive have them read one another's writings and make comments. They are comfortable using the tablets; they have to form their thoughts in writing, a challenge for most of them. I'm hoping as a result they will not choose to encamp in their own points of view and not hear the 'other side,' which is so prevalent in today's society."

"I liked Mr. J's phrase, 'grounded in reality,'" said Gordon. "I've noticed, especially in history textbooks, obsolete information. We owe it to teach students to recognize facts from fiction. It can be easy to allow the first bytes heard or read to become enough. Sometimes we let headlines tell the story and do not read through an article for the whole perspective. And I think of the impact of Fox News's claim to be 'fair and balanced' while at the same time violating this principle—especially in its evening segments."

"However, maybe I'll show one of their news shows—and other cable shows—and see what transpires. It may not be politically correct to do that in a classroom," Gordon added, "but I'll take my chances. Besides, I agree that we must engage in teaching students how to assess TV and the Internet. Not to do so would be irresponsible."

Bonnie jumped in, "Mr. J taught in a time free of meeting standards and outside tests, but I liked how he took charge of his teaching. As you know, the universe story piece has set me thinking. While I may be expected to follow the science curriculum, I intend to bring this story into the early part of the course. My students need to be aware of the interconnectivity of everything, including the Big Bang and the 'flaring forth' of the universe—Brian Swimme's term—which is key for this understanding."

Amy smiled agreeing with Bonnie's decision. "I, too, fully intend to make the curriculum my own even if it's someone else's directive. I will take advantage of what we all know but rarely state: We have a freedom behind the closed door of our classrooms. We can be the teachers we want and need to be. No one has been in my room since the first day; I doubt anyone will bother to come unless they tell me ahead of time—and of course only to evaluate me.

"My students are already sensing that I'm taking charge and that I'm open to their input. I wonder what an evaluator would say about my approach, but I will never perform a dog-and-pony show. If I play the conformist game, doing what others do to stay in the cadre of fellow teachers, I would give up my integrity. It's not worth it."

Bonnie said, "I remember my teachers who seemed to go through the motions. The ones who had the same routine every class: collecting homework, teaching the next concept in the textbook, letting students start their next homework assignment before the bell. I don't intend to do that. Rather, I pay attention to what I am doing, to its effect, and how well I'm achieving my expectations. It's essential to be self-aware. It would be easier simply to come into school, do my job, and go home—to go from day to day without much thought. So much of the day is regulated, scheduled, that it takes lots of energy to keep up and deal with all the distractions. I intend to be my own kind of teacher."

"You can say that again, Bonnie!" said Amy. "Already we endure at least one message a day from the office over the PA, periodic calls from guidance or nurse's office, fire drills, janitors vacuuming halls, and lawn mowers outside our windows. I'm going to send Mr. J an email and ask how he coped in with these distractions in his day."

To shift the conversation, Gordon brought up what he felt was the centerpiece of Mr. J's classroom: the quality of engagement. "You can see from his examples that he made every effort to stay deep inside his material. I can't imagine him being a deliverer. I see him as an inquisitor of the subject and of his students' minds. It would be hard to be passive in his classes. I intend my level best to engage my students when I have to use the textbook, and if possible incorporate information from other textbooks for comparison. We will try to determine which account is closest to the truth. Better than just the one textbook! I may try this!"

"And along those lines," said Amy, "is Mr. J's enthusiasm, his commitment. As I've said, he's convinced me to build respect by listening. I intend, as well, to bring my enthusiasm into the room and make it obvious. Maybe that will entice my kids to come on board, at least some of them. We'll see."

"I agree," said Gordon. Bonnie nodded as well. "I came into teaching wanting to change the world. Well, not quite. But I want to offer the best I have. I can't do any less. My kids seem to be looking for something to grab onto. I observe them isolated on their phones in corridors and outside of school. I want to show them ways to interact, listen, converse! I intend my math classes to come alive! Mr. J did not have to face digital distractions, but I'll bet he'd be right there with me. He made it a priority to connect with each one of his kids.

"And when you think about it, it was never enough to learn something without creating a context. I remember wasting time in classes where I was expected to take notes and later regurgitate them on a quiz or test. I wish I had been in his classroom. I sense the power of his pursuit of meaning in the universe story. I've known only a few teachers like that. I intend to be one."

With that comment, Amy Watson, Gordon Mason, and Bonnie Canton called it a night. They were grateful for Mr. J's insights. They felt geared up for the fight to be good teachers, to meet the challenges of their digital teenagers—and never to give up.

NOTES

1. See YouTube, *Carl Sagan Cosmos Intro* to watch this seminal moment with just the right music in U.S. television.
2. Brian Swimme, *Canticle to the Cosmos* (DVD, 1990).
3. Brian Thomas Swimme and Mary Evelyn Tucker, *Journey of the Universe* (New Haven, CT: Yale University Press, 2011).
4. Brian Swimme and Thomas Berry, *The Universe Story: From the Primordial Flaring Forth to the Ecozoic Era—A Celebration of the Unfolding of the Cosmos* (New York: HarperCollins, 1992).
5. Ken Wilber, *A Brief History of Everything* (Boston: Shambhala, 1996), 20.
6. Swimme and Berry, op. cit., 74.
7. Ibid., 71–73.
8. Ron Fricke, director, *Baraka*, 1992.

Chapter 15

Seek the Middle Ground

Martin Oldenberg, Ellen Harper, Isabella Gonzalez, and Thomas Singleton

In movies we forget about the world around us. We lock into what's happening.

It had been two months since Ellen Harper and Isabella Gonzalez met with Mr. Oldenberg. In a long conversation with her new colleague, Thomas Singleton, Ellen expressed her desire to inspire better listening in her students who tended to stubbornly hold onto set points of view, which inhibited their having conversations.

Thomas, a head taller than Ellen, wore black-rimmed glasses and had an animated face beneath his curled brown hair. "I see the same in my students. I do not remember that happening when I was in school. We need to do something about it."

Ellen suggested that he join her and Isabella Gonzalez the following Saturday to meet with Mr. Oldenberg at the Blanton Café. "If you come, you're in for a treat."

"I'll be there."

The three young teachers found their veteran colleague with his cappuccino and croissant at a corner table. Ellen introduced Thomas to the controversial veteran. She ordered a green tea, Isabella a latte, and Thomas an Americano. Ellen explained to Mr. Oldenberg that she and Thomas were having difficulty facilitating discussions around controversial topics. Students tended to present opinions expecting everyone to agree with them. When they didn't, they retreated further into their points of view. Any thought of reaching consensus was unimaginable. She wanted to hear from Mr. Oldenberg on how to have kids discuss without forming armed camps.

"I am not surprised, Ellen, that you brought this up," said Mr. Oldenberg. "I, too, have had more difficulty recently engaging with my students. They seem to prefer to build walls around their thinking. However, I can offer some approaches to help all of us. I'll begin with Peter Elbow. I met him at a workshop in the mid-1980s. I'm a devotee of his book *Embracing Contraries: Explorations in Learning and Teaching*.[1] I highly recommend it when you have time. It is a challenging read but worth it. I am a big fan of two of Elbow's concepts: 'methodological belief' and 'methodological doubt.' Fancy terms, I admit, but useful as you'll see.

"I imagine the three of you have undoubtedly tried different techniques to make conversation. Likely, you've asked students to search for common ground on issues to find points of agreement. You probably try to have the conversation build out in search for more commonality, but this is not easy to make happen. Peter Elbow offers steps to get there.

"Let me begin with his methodological belief. Elbow stumbled on this concept as a game: 'Each participant promises to try to believe what the others see in return for the others trying to believe what she sees.'[2] Think about this." Mr. Oldenberg paused. "It does not ask people to present an argument, to prove their point, to win—in essence evoking methodological doubting. Instead, Elbow invites people to listen, to experience what the speaker's saying, to build on her vision. Listening is a way of seeing, of experiencing, not arguing.

"One of Elbow's big ideas is not to reject an idea until you have succeeded in believing it. But Elbow adds, you do not have to act on this newly discovered belief. In the meantime, you will have taken a deep look into a different viewpoint. I like to think this process makes for better listening and greater empathy with those with whom we disagree. But it's more challenging now in today's political climate. All the more reason to invoke Elbow's thinking."

"I connect with what you're saying, Mr. Oldenberg," said Thomas. "I've tried to get my kids to take seriously other people's points of view but with little success. I think I am doing it from the wrong posture: As each student defends his position, I require others to listen and not interrupt, but I can see that they are waiting for their turn to insert their arguments."

"I know that process," added Isabella. "I've tried it, and after a while I simply gave up. Hearing an oppositional point of view reaches the brain stem first, the place of fight or flight. We need to find ways for conversations to move to the amygdala, better yet to the frontal cortex. Then we might have reasonable exchanges."

"You make good points, Thomas and Isabella," said Mr. Oldenberg. "Let me continue with Elbow's thinking. When people argue, Elbow contends, they step back, disengage, pause, hold out. They're skeptical and tend to hold on to their position—as you've both recognized. Doubting has its place, as we all know from our education. Taking a position is a baseline of critical thinking and prepares one to defend it with evidence. It has its place, but introducing methodological believing, I believe, can transform your classroom."

"I'm sensing power in Elbow's position," said Ellen. "I can see that my struggles with conversation center around letting doubting to dominate. With doubting, you stand back and view critically; ask tough questions; cite all conceivable reasons why the work (or question) might fall short or fail; and notice problems, faults, or missing pieces—all part of the critical-thinking process. However, I can see that when you believe, you're invited to step inside and try to feel comfortable. You wonder what's interesting or intriguing; what you see when the belief succeeds; under what conditions it might work well; and its strengths. I intend to try this process."

"Yes, Ellen, you're right," said Mr. Oldenberg. "Doubting separates, differentiates, and correlates with individualism; loners hold out and invoke logic to win. Belief moves toward community through finding shared opinions. At the same time—and this may surprise you—Elbow tells us the reverse is also possible: methodological doubt can cement a group, while methodological belief can support individualism and oddball views.[3] As you can see, these distinctions are not simplistic, but for our purposes, let's stick with methodological belief to see how it can make a significant difference in the classroom."

Mr. Oldenberg took a breath. "Teachers are in an ideal position to experiment with believing.[4] We often try something new. Before introducing methodological believing, however, you should practice it. Students sense—even know—when we ask them to do something what we ourselves have not done. Take Elbow's wisdom: 'We seldom see clearly a position or point of view we inhabit till we inhabit one that is genuinely different—not just denial.'[5] You will need to take time to explore this idea for yourselves before you apply it in your classrooms."

"Thomas and Isabella," queried Ellen, "I think we should gather together with a group some Saturday to try this approach. We could do role plays to understand how it feels to believe contrary positions. We could choose topics, such as best approaches to good pedagogy, sex education, or if we dare, today's politics."

"I can assure you," said Isabella, "we'll certainly have a spectrum of opinions in the school on these and other topics."

"And I'll be glad to participate," said Mr. Oldenberg. "I know some colleagues who would join us." Mr. Oldenberg reached into his briefcase and passed out a list he'd drawn from Elbow to facilitate understanding his process:

- Invoke the five-minute rule: Allow one who's feeling she's not getting a fair hearing five uninterrupted minutes with no criticism—and a commitment to try to believe.
- Try to say "yes" to something you're having trouble believing; this may get you into the door.
- Think of believing as an effort to understand.
- Don't be uptight in the process; relax, see it as a game; no high stakes here.
- And use questions to help people get into the process. Elbow suggests:
  - What's interesting and helpful about the view? What are some of the intriguing features that others might not have noticed?
  - What would you notice if you believed in this view? If it were true?
  - In what senses or under what conditions might this idea be true?[6]

"I think I'm getting it," said Isabella. "I can't wait to practice. I've spent most of my life with a tendency to be defensive. Perhaps I'll become better at opening up to others' points of view."

Thomas chimed in, "I'm with you Isabella. I can already see a different classroom in the making. I really want to break down the barriers that shut down listening, being reinforced in the daily political divisiveness in our country."

Ellen said, "I've been preparing my kids to have better conversations. I have them restate what a classmate says before offering another opinion. The first student has to acknowledge that his idea has been restated correctly before the conversation continues. It takes time, demands paying attention, but encourages them to listen to each other. It slows the pace but is well worth it. Adding methodological believing to mix will make a positive difference."

"I'm impressed, Ellen," said Mr. Oldenberg. "I've used your technique, but I've not required approval from the first speaker. Thanks for that idea. I have a couple more thoughts from Elbow for you three to consider. The first concerns freewriting. He has students take three minutes to write nonstop in answer to a question. For instance, 'What's the role of religion in your life?' Or, 'How well do you think the president is doing?' 'What makes for a good person?'

"The point, Elbow emphasizes, is to write nonstop. No thinking, no editing, simply write. This process brings ideas to mind, which become fodder for discussion. It frees people to become open. I've done it and watched how it releases the flow of discussion.

"The second concerns listening. I know the three of you understand its importance. How would it be possible to have conversations in which people don't listen? Listening is basic to all we've been discussing. Yet you tell me that you struggle to get your kids to listen well. You say they seem distracted even when their phones are put away.

"Rebecca Shafir, a speech-language pathologist, has written a profound book, one you should read, called *The Zen of Listening*.[7] Of all the sound arguments she makes, an idea that she learned from a client works for me: people need to listen to one another as if they are in a movie. In movies we forget about the world around us. We lock into what's happening. When we leave, we've been affected, perhaps changed a bit. This is what Shafir calls Zen listening: needing to be in the moment, letting go of self, being mindful, focusing on the process and totally absorbed.[8]

"Think about that. How do kids learn to listen? Hopefully from their parents. But when they come into our classrooms distracted, we have to do this task. I've been a believer that actions speak louder than words. For them to learn to listen, we need to listen to them. I suggest that we follow up on Ellen's practice of having a student repeat what another student has just said to that student's satisfaction before continuing the conversation, and I don't mean repeating every answer to our questions. When we allow a student to elaborate her thoughts, we show that we are listening. Teachers are role models after all."

"What a great idea," said Thomas. "I'm ready to do this in my own life. My wife and I often converse with phones in our hands. No way do I listen fully, nor does she. I hope I can change this practice at home so we can listen better. I came into teaching thinking I had to tell important stuff. Perhaps I should devote at least half the time to listen to what my students have to say. I would come home learning at least as much as I taught!" Isabella and Ellen couldn't agree more.

"Let me end this part of our conversation," Mr. Oldenberg said, "by sharing a quotation from Lewis Carroll's *Through the Looking Glass*":

"I can't believe that!" said Alice.

"Can't you?" said the Queen in a pitying tone. "Try again; draw a long breath, and shut your eyes."

Alice laughed. "There's no use trying," she said, "one *can't* believe impossible things."

"I daresay you haven't had much practice," said the Queen. "When I was your age, I always did it for half-an-hour a day. Why sometimes I believed as many as six impossible things before breakfast!"[9]

"Amen," said Ellen.

"I know implementing Elbow's methodological belief will be a challenge," Mr. Oldenberg said with a glint in his eye. "Forging your path takes courage as you make it your own. I discovered early on that I did not need to replicate the patterns of my forebears, nor of my veteran colleagues. I wanted to commingle with my students rather than talk at them. Not because I wanted to win friendships—good when it happened—but to be the creative adult in the room. And as I stressed the last time we met, we need to seek strong relationships with our students. Implementing methodological belief may help you do that.

"And look for ideas far from the structure of traditional curriculum. Whenever I bring something fresh into my classroom, everyone perks up. It's as if I'm not 'the teacher' but a person with ideas waiting to hear from them. They see me as not as a purveyor of information but as an inquisitive person. That's why I remain fresh all these years and have never burned out. Unlike colleagues who look forward to the last bell on Friday, I look forward to Mondays."

Mr. Oldenberg took a deep breath and suggested they take a break and get another coffee. He got his cappuccino, Ellen her green tea, Isabella another latte, and Thomas this time, a cappuccino. They settled back in their chairs. Mr. Oldenberg, folding his arms and leaning back, resumed the conversation. "Returning to methodological believing, it did not always work for me. Some groups—and increasingly in these last years—struggle to get there. Then I discovered Edward de Bono's *Six Thinking Hats*.[10]

"Imagine reading de Bono's first sentence: 'The Six Thinking Hats method may well be the most important change in human thinking for the past twenty-three hundred years.'[11] Such arrogance, I thought! What writer would ever claim to have written 'the most important book'? Well, I decided to give de Bono a chance. After we discuss his six hats, you can decide for yourselves.

"Here's a brief summary of his six hats; let me read them":

- White Hat: neutral and objective, concerned with facts and figures, data
- Red Hat: the emotional point of view, intuition
- Black Hat: careful and cautious, devil's advocate, the skeptic's hat, risks
- Yellow Hat: sunny and positive, sees potential in good things, benefits
- Green Hat: color of growing things, originality, novel insights, creativity
- Blue Hat: color of the sky, above everything else, the organizing hat, process

For the next twenty minutes Mr. Oldenberg led a discussion of the qualities and merits of each of the six hats and the six-hat process in the classroom. The three young teachers became intrigued about its potential.

Isabella spoke first. "What I like is that everyone gets to wear each hat, each hat being equivalent. Instead of arguing to reach a conclusion, everyone contributes to create a full picture, like a full-color print. No one will be trying to win; everyone will be looking to reach a conclusion, possibly a consensus."

"It's like working in tandem," said Ellen, "what de Bono calls 'parallel thinking,' in which everyone works to 'unbundle thinking,' another de Bono term you explained, Mr. Oldenberg. With the six hats, students won't be tempted to become defensive and will be more open to Elbow's methodological believing process."

"I can't tell you how excited I am about this process," said Thomas, eager to share. "I can see my guys struggling at first having to try on all six hats. I'm thinking of my student, Ishmael, a skeptic who questions everything; how will he wear the yellow hat? I like that donning a thinking hat is natural, like putting on a piece of clothing or taking it off. I might ask my students, 'Are there anymore green hat ideas? If not, let's switch to the white hat.'

"Wearing a hat is taking on a role: 'Wearing my teacher hat, let me say . . .'; 'wearing my parent hat, I want to let you know . . .'. It will be like playing a game," Thomas said gleefully. "Everyone participates. Everyone can wear any hat. No need to be negative: 'Oh, so you are wearing the black hat.' I can't wait to use them!"

"It's like playing golf, one of my favorite sports," said Mr. Oldenberg, "where you use all the clubs in your bag: a driver for long shots, a putter on the green. Each of the six hats has a specific function. As de Bono wrote":

> Every thinker should be able to use each hat just as every golfer should be able to use each club. It is true that some people may be better at one hat than another. Some people may also prefer to use one hat rather than another. But the hats do not represent descriptions of thinkers. Each hat specifies a direction and focus for thinking.[12]

"I've used his words as a reminder of why I like six-hat thinking in my classroom," Mr. Oldenberg said with a smile.

"I like de Bono's simplicity," said Isabella. "I can see my kids grasping the qualities of each hat, although they may struggle at first. Putting on a particular hat modifies behavior without having to judge it. Wearing a hat can empower a student to speak openly without fear; she is playing a role after all. And putting on hats encourages cooperation—one of Elbow's goals—and enhances the quality of thinking. I think I'll introduce them, one hat at a time, until I feel we are ready to use them." Both Ellen and Thomas nodded in agreement.

"Now you can see why I adopted the six hats," said Mr. Oldenberg. "My own skepticism at first (black hat) about de Bono and my emotional reaction (red hat) to his initial claim, became an investigation of its merits (white hat). My kids and I came up with creative ideas (green hat) with some eagerly supporting (yellow hat), all of it in an organized, efficient process (blue hat). I came to agree with de Bono's conclusion at the end of his preface":

The effectiveness of the method is much greater than I had ever imagined. It is an alternative to the argument system (e.g., Socrates, Plato, and Aristotle), which was never intended to be constructive or creative. With the Six Hats method the emphasis is on "what can be" rather than on what "what is," and how we design a way forward—not who is right and who is wrong.[13]

"My initial reaction to de Bono reminded me that I need to suspend judgment until I understand what I am looking at. I pride myself on knowing, but value asking questions to get there. I pay attention to what I hear or read and acknowledge newfound evidence. Bad habits are hard to break. Humility is a good place to start." Reaching into his briefcase, Mr. Oldenberg pulled out a copy of *Six Thinking Hats* for each of his protégés. There were smiles all around.

With that, the four got up from the table, and the three younger teachers thanked Mr. Oldenberg. He in turn, thanked them for being willing to have this conversation. "I am privileged," he concluded, "to help you launch your journeys into this great profession. Regardless of what you hear from parents or the public, know that you are the backbone of your school. You are the ones who spend time with the children. You may be closer to them than their parents. Don't forget that."

NOTES

1. Peter Elbow, *Embracing Contraries: Explorations in Learning and Teaching* (New York: Oxford University Press, 1986).
2. Ibid., 259.
3. Ibid., 264.
4. Ibid., 274.
5. Ibid., 268.
6. Ibid., 275.
7. Rebecca Z. Shafir, *The Zen of Listening: Mindful Communication in the Age of Distraction*, 2nd ed. (Wheaton, IL: Quest Books, 2003).
8. Ibid., chapter 5, "What Is Their Movie?," 81–102.
9. Elbow, *Embracing Contraries*, 254.
10. Edward de Bono, *Six Thinking Hats* (New York: Little, Brown and Company, 1985).
11. Ibid., ix.
12. http://www.debonothinkingsystems.com/tools/6hats.htm.
13. de Bono, *Six Thinking Hats*, xiii.

Chapter 16

And It's the Little Things

Lillian Bailey, Michael Harding, Meera Sharma, John Hutchinson, Ford Daley, and Martha Esersky

And in the beginning was not a Word, but a chirrup.

Meera Sharma had been surprised and delighted with her meetings with Michael Harding at the Witney Café. His wisdom, cultivated a generation before her, proved invaluable. She has a better grasp of her purpose and of practical approaches—taking her desks out of rows was the first. Despite having digitally focused students, so different from Mr. Harding's and from her own schooling, his ideas have proved invaluable. She was grateful to stand on his shoulders.

In the spring of her first year, she thought back to her high school and remembered Lillian Bailey, her favorite English teacher. Meera discovered on Facebook that after retirement Ms. Bailey was living in a town not far away. She messaged her and asked if she'd be willing to come to her house to meet with her and some colleagues. Meera wanted her to share the secrets that made her a great teacher. Every third period, Meera had been eager to come to her class. Ms. Bailey agreed to come but did not promise anything.

Ms. Bailey arrived the next Sunday afternoon. Meera led her out to the back terrace where three of her fellow teachers and Michael Harding were waiting. "Ms. Bailey, I want you to meet Michael Harding, the man I told you about. These are fellow teachers John Hutchinson, Ford Daley, and Martha Esersky. John and Ford are in the science department; John is in biology, and Ford in basic science. Martha is in the social studies department."

"From what Meera has told us," said Ford, "we are eager to hear about your career." The others nodded.

"Well don't expect too much," Ms. Bailey replied. "I never had a magic wand. I pretty much stayed in my room, and I must say, I loved what I did."

"That was obvious," said Meera. "We always felt that. Hardly a day passed that you didn't smile. I would always leave your class feeling better."

Ford, who could hardly sit still, leaned back in his chair, crossed his legs, flipped back his long hair and peered over his rimless spectacles. Martha, short, wearing a slight frown, leaned forward, and took out her notepad and pen. She had a reputation for her sense of detail and did not want to miss anything. John, the most intense of the three, known for his imaginative labs and sense of order, brought his 35mm camera to capture images of the afternoon.

Ms. Bailey looked at these protégés and thought back to her first days when she was an exuberant twenty-one-year-old. Not much different from them, she thought. Now her hair was white and thinned. She wore the same clear, plastic-rimmed glasses, a white blouse with red roses, blue skirt, and a light-blue cardigan. Despite her years away from the classroom, she seemed to have her intensity and clear focus, and her eyes were alive and curious. Meera couldn't wait to get started.

"I'm pleased Meera invited me to speak with you. I hope that I can offer you some useful ideas. Perhaps the best I can do will be to share the little things I discerned over the years. At least they seem little when I discovered them, but many became important. My priority was to connect with each student. From there all else followed. Here's a handout to take home—my goodness, just like I did in my classes! Let me read them aloud and then we can talk":

Buy tickets: This may be the simplest little thing. When you buy tickets, you commit to the event. Few of us ever say, "Never mind, I'm tired and don't want to go." Once in my first year, a colleague and I had tickets for a special performance in a town twenty miles away. That evening a snowstorm was in process. We went anyway.

Celebrate: Being new, you will often find yourself coming up short—at least in your estimation. When you're alone after school, perhaps in your car, first tell yourself what went well that day, what worked, who made you smile, and anything nice your principal or anyone might have said to you. Develop this habit, and you'll begin to think more positively. It's like putting the airline's oxygen mask on first: take care of yourself so you can care for others.

10–2: This idea, an instruction technique from Mary Budd Rowe,[1] woke me up to understand that students cannot listen for long without opportunities to process. Her 10–2 approach showed that when I lectured—I did that a lot at first—I should allow two-minute breaks every ten minutes or so for them to write or talk about what I'd just said. Once I did this, everyone paid better attention, learned more, and did better on tests.[2]

Wait time: This was another instructional gem from Mary Budd Rowe. Wait three seconds for a student to respond (not the usual 0.5) and you'll find that (1) the hesitant ones speak up, (2) full-sentence answers more likely,

(3) higher-order thinking is evident, and (4) more students make comments.[3] At first this is hard—three seconds feels long—but it's well worth it.

Give one/get one: This was a simple exercise I discovered late in my career, which I liked to use for reviewing for tests in class. Instead of going over material, I passed out a sheet with nine empty boxes. First, I asked everyone to write three items at the top they thought should be on the test. Next, they would travel around the room to collect what their classmates thought and put them in the bottom six boxes. When finished, we would process their choices. I found out which items were most on their minds and used them to make the test. I intended my tests to be about what they were learning, not about tricking them.[4]

Treat students as stakeholders: Make them the centerpiece. Invite them in any way you can to take ownership of your classroom.[5] I learned about an idea from Margaret Metzger, a long-time, beloved teacher at Brookline High School: give job assignments for the classroom—from book czar to attendance mogul to Internet whiz to lawyer for the defense. Each kid had a responsibility (see the Appendix, "Job Assignments in the Classroom," 141).

Make listening your priority: When I went to school, I spent 90 percent of my time sitting and listening to teachers. They were charged with giving knowledge and did their best to have us take it all in. But this method did not serve my kids well. They were eager to express ideas, to hear from each other. So one day I said to myself: less from me, more from them.

Meera raised her hand. "In my first meeting with Mr. Harding, he told me about putting his desks in a horseshoe to improving listening and conversation. How right he proved to be. And I remember how often, Ms. Bailey, you stood still patiently listening, not only from the front of the room. I did not realize how important that was to you, but I surely appreciated it."

Step aside: I wish I knew this concept early in my career. As a young teacher, I would find myself being unjustly berated by a supervisor or parent. A veteran told me in that case to simply step aside and look at where I was standing and say to myself, "That's not me." I listen but I know I am better than that; I am a good teacher, a good person. Remember to separate yourself from that "you" who's being berated.[6]

Count backward: A simple suggestion with powerful repercussions. When you sense an oncoming conflict, pause, count back slowly from ten—or from twenty if you feel you have to. Recompose yourself. Your response will not only benefit you but everyone. Let students know what you are doing if they are curious.

Personal care: Eat well, exercise, and sleep. Take time for yourself. Do nothing. Need I say more?

The emergency lesson: Few teachers get through each year without being ill or having to take personal leave. Having emergency lessons in a specified file for substitutes allows you to be away without having to scramble to devise on-the-spot lessons. Two or three in a folder may be all you'll need; the office secretary can show the substitute.

Don't take anything personally: This is the second agreement from Don Miguel Ruiz, *The Four Agreements*.[7] Of the four, this one tells you to see the world as not about you. Each person acts as who he is. What people say to or do to you belongs to them, not you. I suggest that you read his book. In case you're curious, Ruiz's other three agreements are these: Be impeccable with your word, don't make assumptions, and always do your best. Not a bad list if you ask me.

Mental health days: As you know, teaching can be stressful. Curricula goals to meet, papers and tests to correct, an angry parent, a sudden schedule shift, unexpected criticism, a fire drill, meetings upon meetings. You know how these can get to you. A colleague suggested that we take mental health days. Simply "call in well," a saying attributed to author Tom Robbins. I did it a couple of times and my stress level dropped precipitously. I highly recommend it.

Know names: I discovered in my first year the importance of using names. Greeting students as they come in, sometimes stand at the door, greet by name, perhaps saying something good you heard about them; again say "good-bye" at the door. I was anxious to have good relationships with each student, no exceptions. Sometimes, a student who was not doing well, my connection with her would make a difference. Not always, but I never gave up.

Ask for help I: When I was a pupil, I saw my teachers do everything. I thought they knew all they needed to know, because I rarely saw them conferring with other teachers except for having coffee in the teacher's room. But when I started to teach, I discovered when I asked for help from colleagues, administrators, parents—and students!—I became a better teacher.

Ask for help II: In my later years, the Internet appeared. I discovered, as you no doubt know, that I had direct access to the outside world. I'd subscribed to education magazines, but did not always find time to read them. Then I discovered two sources, both still around, that became invaluable:

Marshall Memo[8]: Kim Marshall has published over seven hundred weekly issues, each issue gleaned from sixty-four sources summarizing some of the best thinking in education. His cogent, focused writing offers teachers information on crucial matters in all fields—and recently on the role of cellphones.

The Main Idea[9]: Jenn David-Lange is one of the brightest people in our field. She composes eight-to-ten-page summaries of books and short reviews of what she deems as good ideas and methods to improve schools. And she provides exercises to process some of the books.

I urge you to consider these publications, not only for yourselves but for your department or school. The more who subscribe, the cheaper the cost—and the greater potential for lively staff discussions!

Kindness: Practice the power of gratitude. You will never run out of chances to say thank you: to students without whom you would not have a job; to the office who keeps your school running; to janitors who keep your room and the school clean; to colleagues from all departments; to administrators who do much behind-the-scene work; and to parents. Every time I said thank you, I connected to the world around me. It's easy to do—and it's free! It helped me to see the positive side even in tough times.

"And may I leave you with a quotation that has been at the heart of my teaching. Listen and think how it might speak to you":

> Brute force crushes many plants. Yet the plants rise again. Pyramids will not last a moment compared to the daisy. And before Buddha or Jesus spoke the nightingale sang, and long after Buddha and Jesus are gone into oblivion the nightingale still will sing. Because it is neither preaching nor teaching nor commanding nor urging. It is just singing. And in the beginning was not a Word, but a chirrup.[10]

Meera was thrilled. Her beloved English teacher had come to her home and shared some of her insights. Conversation was animated, Mr. Harding and Ms. Bailey leading the way. Ford was thrilled to learn about 10–2, something he intended to use the next Monday for his introductory lecture on chemistry. Martha liked having the open door to ask for help; she had been carrying the notion that she would have to figure everything out for herself. And John, taking it all in, took several photos, including a close-up of Ms. Bailey that he wanted to put by his desk to remind him of his afternoon at Meera's.

"If I were not convinced," said Meera, "now I know how important it is to learn from teachers before me." The other three young teachers agreed. And they intended to seek out others for ideas and advice. "You can't do it alone," said Meera. "You can't do it alone."

NOTES

1. Saphier and Gower, *The Skillful Teacher*, 219.
2. See Frank Thoms, *Exciting Classrooms: Practical Information to Ensure Student Success* (Lanham, MD: Rowman & Littlefield, 2015), chapter 1, 78, 113.
3. Saphier and Gower, *The Skillful Teacher*, 309.
4. Thoms, *Exciting Classrooms*, 40–43.
5. Ibid., chapter 23.
6. I learned about this idea from Greg Ciardi in my first year as a consultant.
7. Don Miguel Ruiz, *The Four Agreements: A Practical Guide to Personal Freedom* (San Rafael, CA: Amber-Allen Publishing, 1997).
8. *Marshall Memo*, https://www.marshallmemo.com.
9. *The Main Idea*, http://themainidea.net.
10. D. H. Lawrence, *Sketches of Etruscan Places and Other Italian Essays*, edited by Simonetta De Filippis (Cambridge: Cambridge University Press, 2002), 36.

Coda

"You see?" he said smiling. "We both know it's impossible. But it doesn't matter, as long as we believe it might be possible one day."[1]

"You can't do it alone." These were the first words of this book. You can't. You've chosen a profession that demands more than others understand. You've chosen to care for the young, to be a beacon, to be an inspiration, to be a counselor—in essence, to be a teacher. In *Listening Is Learning*, you've met some remarkable teachers from both the twentieth and twenty-first centuries. You've observed the value of conversation, of listening, of being present to one another.

Your predecessors faced students who were much like they were when they went to school. You, on the other hand, face young people who are different from you, who have a different social context. Many arrive distracted, addicted to their phones, alone for hours on their screens. Yet teaching is teaching, the work and responsibilities are the same: to meet challenges, seek engagement, ask questions, build relationships, enact conversations, be fair, invoke learning, accept change, and much more.

Teaching is enormously complex, a challenge that invites deep participation. Discouragement awaits but can be superseded by persistence, acceptance, and hope. Keep in mind the wisdom of master teachers Michael Harding, Frances Smith, Del Goodwin, Don Jorgensen, and young teachers Meera Sharma, Ivan Deutsch, Harold Coughlin, Amy Watson, and others. Let them be your companions as you navigate the challenges of your classrooms. Teaching for this author has been the focus of his life. May the conversations, ideas, and methods in *Listening Is Learning: Conversations between 20th and 21st Century Teachers* inspire you to be the teacher you want to be.

NOTE

1. Willem de Kooning, op. cit.

Appendix

BIOLOGY FINAL EXAM: DAN BISACCIO[1]

More often than not, you will find the definition of *biology* given in a somewhat clinical manner such as, "Biology is the study of life and how organisms relate to their physical environs." However, biologists are in the business of seeking answers to questions, and their search encompasses a much more exciting and broader spectrum than this usual definition implies.

This year you will be the biologist and, in seeking the answers to the questions posed below (and others that will certainly arise), you will have the opportunity to discover and understand a much more comprehensive definition of biology than the one previously stated.

From time to time you will be given the following questions to answer, and, in fact, this is your final exam as well. Each time you answer them, your grade will be based on your development as a biologist. In other words, as the year unfolds, it is expected that you will become more and more the "sophisticated biologist," and your answers should reflect this.

1. Define "biology" in your own words.
2. What characterizes life? In other words: what is the difference between "living" and "non-living"; between "living" and "never-living"?
3. There are five kingdoms of life. What are they? What is common to all? What distinguishes each as a separate kingdom?
4. From a scientific standpoint: how did life begin on this planet? what characteristics of this planet enabled life to evolve? what were some problems early organisms needed to overcome and how did they do it?

5. Within the five kingdoms, biologists recognize millions of species. What is a "species"? Why are there so many different species? In terms of question 4, how did so many forms of life come to be?
6. Perhaps the most essential biochemical reactions are listed below. In terms of entropy (2nd Law of Thermodynamics), discuss the importance of these reactions as they pertain to life:

$$6CO_2 + 6H_2O + SUNLIGHT \rightarrow C_6H_{12}O_6 + 6O_2$$
$$C_6H_{12}O_6 + 6O_2 \rightarrow 6CO_2 + 6H_2O + ENERGY$$

7. In an ecological sense, interpret the essay "Thinking Like a Mountain," written by Aldo Leopold from his book *A Sand County Almanac*:

_____
_____
_____
_____
_____

DUTIES OF SOVIET SCHOOLCHILDREN

It is the duty of every schoolchild:

1. To strive with tenacity and perseverance to master knowledge in order to become an educated and cultured citizen and to serve most full the nation.
2. To be diligent in study and punctual in attendance, never be late to classes.
3. To obey without question the orders of the school director and teachers.
4. To bring to school all necessary books and writing materials, have everything ready before the arrival of the teacher.
5. To appear at school washed, combed, and neatly dressed.
6. To keep his desk in the classroom clean and orderly.
7. To enter the classroom and take his seat immediately after the ringing of the bell, to enter or leave the classroom during the lesson only with the permission of the teacher.
8. To sit erect during the lesson period, not leaning on the elbows or slouching in the seat; to attend closely to the explanation of the teacher and responses of the pupils, not talking or engaging in mischief.

9. To rise as the teacher or the director enters or leaves the classroom.
10. To rise and stand erect while reciting; to sit down only on permission of the teacher; to raise the hand when desiring to answer or ask a question.
11. To make accurate notes of the teacher's assignment for the next lesson, to show these notes to the parents, and to do all the homework without assistance.
12. To be respectful of the school director and the teachers, to greet them on the street with a polite bow, boys removing their hats.
13. To be polite to his elders, to conduct himself modestly or properly in school. on the street, and public places.
14. To abstain from using bad language, from smoking and gamboling.
15. To take good care of school property, to guard well his own possessions and those of his comrades.
16. To be courteous and considerate toward little children, the aged, the weak, and the sick; to give them a seat on the trolley or the right of way on the street; to help them in every way.
17. To obey his parents and assist in the care of little brothers and sisters.
18. To maintain cleanliness in the home by keeping his own clothes, shoes, and bed in order.
19. To carry always his pupil's card, guarding it carefully, not passing it to other children, but presenting it on request of the director or teacher of the school.
20. To prize the honor of his school and his class as his very own.

For violation of these rules the pupil is subject to punishment, even to exclusion from school.[2]

JOB ASSIGNMENTS IN THE CLASSROOM

To: All my students
From: Mrs. Metzger
Re: Job assignments

I need to ask you for a personal favor. Would you be willing to help with small classroom chores? If we can divide the labor, none of the chores is very time consuming; most take under 10 minutes a week. If you are willing to help or if you have special skills, please choose an appropriate task from this list. Tomorrow I will ask you privately if you are willing to do one chore. As a class, you need to nominate a classmate for Attendance Mogul and Lawyer for the Defense. Be sure to check that your nominee is willing to serve. Thank you very much for considering this issue. I appreciate the help.

Chore List

1. *Book Czar*. The Czar checks in and out all the books. The Czar's word is final. If s/he says you owe a book, you do. I'll train the Book Czar to use my record-keeping system. The Czar is the Czar all year.
2. *Attendance Mogul*. This person keeps all attendance records. Again, this person's word is final. I'll explain the school's policies. The Mogul will devise and announce a system for tardiness and errors. The class should choose someone trustworthy for this position.
3. *Two Clerks*. These people assist the Attendance Mogul. The Clerks keep files, collect homework, gather records for recommendations, fill out custodial forms, post deadlines, and coordinate make-up work.
4. *Artist in Residence*. This person makes signs, creates illustrations, draws maps, and produces charts.
5. *Techie*. This person runs machinery, makes tapes, copies videos.
6. *Environmental Designer*. The interior decorator arranges displays, posters, plants, desks, chairs, and, in general, fixes up this room. (Personally, I would like a fireplace, copy machine, and a refrigerator.) We will spend about two hundred hours in this old classroom this year. The Environmental Designer will make our classroom livable.
7. *Luggers*. Luggers bring supplies to the classroom. The book room, illogically, is in the basement, and the classroom is on the fourth floor. The Luggers also run after Xerox copies and supplies. Let's not be sexist: we need two strong girls.
8. *Computer Tutor*. The tutor will help me with the computer. Perhaps for the first time in history, the younger generation has vast knowledge that the older generation doesn't have. As a community of learners, we learn from each other, which includes your teaching me about computers.
9. *Internet Whiz*. This person needs initiative and access to the Internet. I don't even know what might be available to supplement the curriculum. The Whiz should look up the topics we are studying on the Internet. Be creative.
10. *Nag*. Someone with a free period after this class can take two minutes each day to glance around the room and pick up—or nag—other people to do it. Traditionally, women clean up messes; let's have a boy in charge of this.

11. *Barometer*. I need someone in every class to give me feedback. Years ago, a senior boy used to sit in the back and say, "Hey, Metzger, this doesn't make any sense. You think we understand, but we don't. Explain it again." Or: "We did this yesterday, you've got us mixed up with the other class." His comments helped. If the class is feeling overworked or bored or enthusiastic, someone should inform me. The Barometer should also *remind me* if I have forgotten important conflicts between my assignments and your lives, such as the weekend for college boards. Ideally, everyone would be a barometer, but it helps my teaching to have one person assigned to this task.
12. *Host or Hostess*. This person will be gracious to all guests. S/he greets all guests, introduces him or herself, gives the visitor a desk and appropriate handouts, and explains what we are doing in class.
13. *Scrounger*. This resourceful person finds props for plays, materials for demonstrations, and extra copies of books.
14. *Lawyer for the Defense*. Sometimes a class needs to negotiate with me. For example, you may all think a due date needs to be changed. I don't want to talk with all of you *individually*. You need a spokesperson. This needs to be a fair-minded person who will think about the needs of everyone involved (including the teacher). You know each other better than I do. Please choose a mature and fair lawyer to represent you.
15. *C.E.O. (Chief Executive Officer)*. This person oversees everyone else. For example, if the Attendance Mogul is absent, the C.E.O. reminds a Clerk to take over. Ideally, I need someone with the rare skill of being able to walk into a room and figure out what needs to be done. Oldest daughters are sometimes trained in this. Years ago, a freshman used to walk into my room and say things like, "You don't have enough books; you forgot we've got a new kid." Or: "You're missing the adapter for the video: I'll go get it." I was impressed. This extraordinary skill won't get you a job after graduation but it will get you promoted.

The above tasks are minor maintenance chores. Students, your real job is to prepare every day for class, work hard on papers, participate in class, think about the literature and class work, and own your education.

If I can delegate all fifteen tasks for each class, I will concentrate better on my real job: teaching. My central task is to organize knowledge into some reasonable patterns, create learning situations, encourage you to do your best work, give you adult feedback about your performance, and think about how you learn.

Thank you again for your willingness to consider this system. Let's work.

EXAMPLES OF CAPITALIST OPPRESSION

The police: You know what they do? First and foremost, they protect property. Who owns property in a capitalist society? The grande bourgeoisie! Everything they do goes back to protecting property!

And the sanctity of the family! How marvelous it is to be a mother! The family is a unit to keep people happy—an artificial one at that. The family is our opiate, a device to make us forget our troubles, the miseries outside. A place of order and tranquility.

There's the Constitution. Look carefully and you'll see it's a device designed to protect property. That's what judges do. Again, it's the grande bourgeoisie who own property!

In fact, the whole political structure of the United States is a device set up by the grande bourgeoisie to operate for the grande bourgeoisie. Remember, Marx: "Whoever controls the economy, controls the political structure."

(I was relishing sharing how the grande bourgeoisie controlled society. My students, however, were looking at me as if I had pushed the Marxist envelope beyond reality.)

"You don't really believe, Mr. Rowe, that grand bourgeoisie has that much power and control. After all, they are only 0.01 percent of our country. That's not possible!"

"OK, if you don't believe me, look at Hollywood, TV, and radio. Who controls them? The grande bourgeoisie. They own them, as they are devices to keep the people happy. Everybody loves *Gunsmoke* and *The Ed Sullivan Show*. No one is taught to look below the surface to see what might really be going on.

"And then, there's me, your teacher. What's my job? To convince you that you live in the United States, the land of opportunity, where you can get ahead. Education is indoctrination, a device to make the petite bourgeoisie content to be the petite bourgeoisie, the proletariat content to be the proletariat. I am an agent of the grande bourgeoisie. Even if I didn't realize it—you're lucky that I know—it would still be true."

NOTES

1. Fried, *The Passionate Teacher*, 232–33.
2. Stavrianos, *Readings in World History*, 388–89.

Index

10–2, 97, 132, 135
1984 (Orwell), 12

"A, B, and not yet" (Saphier), 55
acknowledge change, 27, 60, 137
addressing attitude, 60
affirmation, 60
The American High School Today (Conant), 5
Animal Farm (Orwell), 10–11, 12, 78–79
Archer, Lea: on books vs. movies, 91; as called to teach, 87–88; curiosity questions by, 90; personal goals for teaching of, 90–91; on smartphones, 89, 93; on teaching first month, 88–89; on teaching getting better, 93–94; on Yondr, 88–89
The Art of Possibility (Zander), 54
ask big questions, 60
ask for help, I & II, 134

backward design mind-set, 26–28
Bailey, Lillian, 131–32, 135
Baraka (Fricke), 118–19
basket for phones, 52, 99, 109

Beck, Charlotte Joko, 19
Becker, Carl, 3, 23
bell curve, 6
Berry, Thomas, 115, 117–18
Bertrand, Joyce: on backward design, 27; intends framework for lessons, 29; invokes Suzuki, 22; on iPads in class, 18, 22; for primary sources, 18; for students as historians, 28; on teaching ancient China, 22; textbook concerns of, 22; use of tablets, Good Drive, 27
Blanton (coffee house), 77, 85, 123
Bodhi, Bhikku, 19
Bonaparte, Napoleon, 6
Booker, Amanda: on department meetings, 101; for emotional intelligence, 99; on former school, 95–96; for Greater Good Science Center, 99; on jigsaw, 97; for lifelong learning, 101; personal philosophy of, 101
Boorstein, Sylvia, 19
British open classroom, 65
Bronstein, Mort, 33, 35, 37, 39
Bruner, Jerome, 62
Buddha, 19, 135;
buy tickets, 132

cadre, 5, 51, 120
Canton, Bonnie: monk-on-the-mountain of, 106, 113; personal expectations of, 120; teaching as calling, 103; on teenagers' phones, 107–109; on texting in homes, 111–12; universe story of, 114, 115, 117, 118, 120; on Wheatley's six principles, 113, 119
capitalism, 37, 46; five laws of, 38; Great Depression in, 38; shortcomings of, 43
Carr, Nicholas, 107
Carroll, Lewis, 127
celebrate, 132
Center for Constructive Change, 25
children, 7, 12, 66, 69; "Boys are . . . Girls are . . ." writing of, 70; on Diplomacy game, 71–72; duties, Soviet, of, 43–44; gym role play by, 71; making choices by, 68; observing to make decisions on, 67; putting first of, 67; screen effect on, 2, 67–68; uninterrupted learning for, 70
The Children's Story (Clavell), 12, 14
China, 34, 61; ancient, 16, 19–20, 22; geography of, 16; history of, 15, 17; Meitu app on, 68; philosophy of, 15; teaching of, 17; textbook on, 16
Chromebooks, 57
Chuang-tzu, 18
classrooms: avoid isolation in, 113; as communities, 88; conversations in (Wheatley) of, 110, 119, 113, 119; cosmic perspective in, 114–15; disciplined aim of, 67; of engaging, 41, 113; Facebook, Google, effect in, 109; on flipped, 16; on freedom behind closed door, 120; grounded in reality in, 109, 114, 115, 116, 119; about ideal, 29; for immersion, 11, 37, 41; as inner sanctum, 36; learning happens in, 12, 23, 54, 68, 125; *Main Idea* for, 132; *Marshall Memo* for, 134; mediation practice in, 70; no smartphones in, 7, 61, 69, 88; open, 66, 77; personal approach to, 1, 2; protective privacy in, 5; of simulated Soviet, 44–48; SMART board use in, 22, 37, 39, 61; South American festival of, 36; as symphonies, 117–18; on traditional curriculum, 76; on Yondr, 88–89
Clavell, James, 12, 14
Cold War, 41; *The Children's Story*, 12; teaching (Rowe) about, 35–39
collaboration: activities for children of, 68; for backward design, 27; I/D/I in, 73; iPad use for, 37, 63; open classroom of, 66
commitment: to be a unique teacher, 5; to Bruner hypothesis, 62; by conservatory A students, 54; emotional in Backward design of, 27; on *Iskra* reporters excellence, 47; to reading and writing, 51; to real information, 109; in teaching, 10, 22, 121; to try to believe, 126; wakeup call to, 88
Common Core, 80
Communist Manifesto (Marx and Engels), 11, 39
community: classroom loss of, 71; Diplomacy banquet as, 72; Sangha (Buddha), 19; teachers as members of, 80; "The Meeting" as, 20–21; through methodological belief, 125
Conant, James, 5
Confucius, 21; analects of, 16–19, 22; filial piety of, 16; philosophy of, 16, 62
Cosmic Calendar (Sagan), 116–17
Cosmos (Sagan), 114–15, 117, 121n1
cossacks, 44
Coughlin, Harold: on challenges in teaching, 101; for emotional intelligence, 99; get out of yourself of, 101; lack of empathy in students, 97; on letters from students, 54; on power of threat, 56; teaching

frustrations of, 51–52; on teaching well, 56–57
count backward, 133
The Courage to Teach: Exploring the Inner Landscape of a Teacher's Life (Palmer), 60
critical thinking: intention to teach, 38; methodological doubt and, 124–25; for test prep, 44
cubbies for phones, 4, 39–40, 63, 67, 76, 89, 109
curiosity: engage, 14, 39–40, 78, 95, 115; lack of, 10, 51, 88, 89–90; questions for, 90
cyberbullying, 97, 108

Dalai Lama, 19
Daley, Ford, 131–32, 135
David-Lange, Jenn, 134
de Bono, Edward, 128–30
Denton, Lewis: co-teach offer from Mr. Goodwin, 59–60; on good teaching, 60; letter about Mr. Goodwin, 61–63; letter from Jeremy Wilson, 65–74;
depressed kids, 2
desks in horseshoe, 7, 9, 10, 133
Deutsch, Ivan: duties of Soviet school children of, 43; ideas for teaching, 39; on motivation to teach, 34; on Mr. Rowe, 39, 44; on preconditions of socialism, 37, 41; preparation to teach, 34; on teaching Russia, 49
dialectical materialism, 37
digital devices: as becoming the norm, 106, 107, 116; challenge of, 74, 121; cyberbullying with, 108; as distractions, 10, 99, 121; excessive app use of, 4, 108; lack of students' vocabulary, 88; in separating people, 74; shift to conversations away from, 108–109; time way from peers of, 88; uses in class of, 2, 29, 61, 68, 78
Diplomacy, 71–73
discussions, 7, 33, 68, 88

displays of students work, 73
dog-and-pony show, 54, 78, 120
don't take anything personally, 134
dress rehearsal, last great, 55

Ehrenreich, Barbara, 51
Elbow, Peter, 124–28, 129
Embracing Contraries: Explorations in Learning and Teaching (Elbow), 124
embracing controversy, 76–85
emergency lesson, 133–34
emotional intelligence (EQ), 98–99
empathy, 97–99; as human quality, 21; inculcate in students, 97; less of, in children, 97; for, others, 124; smartphone effect on, 97; for Soviet children, 44
emperor is not wearing any clothes, 15, 85
engagement, 71, 137; for 10–2, 132, 135; backward design and, 27; challenge of screened-in kids, for, 63; create aspirations for, 95; emotional intelligence for, 98–99; give one/get one for, 133; in the minds of students, 23; primary sources for, 18; problem solving for, 57; quality of classroom, 2, 120; to raise curiosity in students, 14, 39–40, 115; reading Solzhenitsyn for, 92; students hungry for, 74; testing's lack of, 56
"Enthusiasm March," 45–46
Esersky, Martha, 131–32, 135

face-to-face teaching: in conversation, 37, 109, 119; Del Goodwin about, 61; in ideal classroom, 29; for interactive learning, 68, 88, 97
feedback: on collegial, 91; on parent, 54; piano teacher, 12; on teacher (Zander), 54
fixed mind-set, 63

flipped classroom, at Kahn Academy, 16
Florida-Cuba Dam, 13
The Four Agreements (Ruiz), 134
freedom behind the closed door, 120
freewriting (Elbow), 126
Fricke, Ron, 118

give one/get one, 132
Gladwell, Malcolm, 51
The Golden Compass (Pullman), 69
Golding, William, 12
Gonzalez, Isabella: on conversations, 124; for methodological believing, 126, 129; on Mr. Oldenberg, 76, 80; phone cubbies, 76; for six-hat thinking, 128, 129; on traditional curriculum, 76
Goodwin, Del: for Bruner's hypothesis, 62; co-teach invitation to Lewis Denton, 59; description of, 61–63; on Dweck's *fixed* and *growth* mind-set, 63; high standards of, 62; on stock exchange, 62; as throwback, 61; trust in Lewis Denton, 61–62
Google, 105–106, 107, 109–110, 111, 119; Drive, 27, 119; Maps, 106
grading rubric, 56
grande bourgeoisie, 38, 48
Grapes of Wrath (Steinbeck), 51
Greater Good Science Center, Berkley, 98–99
growth mindset, 63, 100
guidance office, 6, 52–53, 120

Hagen, Steve, 19
Hahn, Thich Nhat, 18, 19
Hamlet (Shakespeare), 88, 94
Harding, Michael: for backward design, 26–27; being unique, 6; for big rocks, 30; on cadres, 5; childhood of, 9–10; on *The Children's Story*, 12; for desks in horseshoe, 9; for engaging material, 10; on fairness to students, 4–5; first year teaching of, 3–6; on ideal classroom, 29; on ideal doorman, 25, 29; on path to teaching, 2–3; piano teacher metaphor, 12; on protective privacy of classroom, 5; punning of, 10; reflection on tracking, 12–14; seeds from childhood of, 5; on taking the long view, 25–26; on teaching *Animal Farm*, 10–11; textbooks, opposition to, 5; as tough grader, 6; as young elite, 5
Harper, Ellen: on better conversations, 126; on better listening in students, 123; concern about phones, 76; on contacting parents, 79; on favorite social teacher, 77; on her first day of school, 75; grounded in reality of, 85; methodological believing of, 125; on sequencing lessons, 79; for six-hat thinking, 129; student teaching of, 76
"Have Smartphones Destroyed a Generation?" (Twenge), 1
Hawkins, David, 67
Hench, Carolyn: conversation, honor to have, 93; Google's instant searches of, 90; for reading engagement, 89, 91–92; on role plays, 91–92; soundbite culture of, 90; students as honored guests of, 93–94; teaching, reflection on her years, 87
high standards, 62–63
Hitler, Adolf, 36
Hoban, Russell, 69, 80–81
Hoff, Benjamin, 18
home groups, 68–69
homework: as dinner conversations, 13, 104; equal for students, 4; as none given, 104; pig stamps with, 11; questioning about doing, 53; routine of, 5, 78, 120; for thinking in, 90
honored guests mind-set, 93
Hutchinson, John, 131–32, 135

I Have a Dream/Letter from Birmingham Jail (King), 51–52
ideal doorman, 25, 29
iGen generation, 1
immersion classroom, 37, 41
Informed Vision: Essays on Learning and Human Nature (Hawkins), 67
initiating/designing/implementing (I/D/I) planning method, 73
internet: as access to world, 37, 39, 90, 91; accessing/how to use, 108, 120; arrival of, 105; big rocks in, 30; faux-internet sites, 90; internet-speak, 81; shallowness of, 107
iPad: carts on, 2, 18, 22, 39; in-class, 37, 63; planbook for, 56
Iskra (newspaper), 45–49

Jervis, Fred, 25
Jorgensen, Don (Mr. J): on ancient history teaching, 104, 114; conversations (Wheatley) of, 110, 111; on creationism, 113–14; on grounded in reality, 109, 114, 115; language usage of students, 105–106; monk-on-the-mountain problem, of, 104–105, 106, 111, 115; philosophy at waiter's table, 106; on phone use, 107, 109, 111; teachers as deciders, 109; on universe story, 114–18

Keltner, Dacher, 98
Kennedy, John F., 13
Khrushchev, Nikita, 44, 46–48; portrayed as, 46–47
kindness: as gratitude, 134; quality of, 21, 98; random acts of, 97–98; as self-compassionate letter, 98; as stream of water, 18; teacher having, 66, 97
King, Martin Luther, Jr., 51

Lao Tzu, 18
laptops: avoid in class, 7; oppression of, 95–96
learning in the classroom: conversations through, 7; grounded in reality, not belief, for, 114; life process through, 23; on methodical belief, 125; more learning occurs when, 12; *Six Thinking Hats* for, 128–30; students' stake in, 54; teachers responsible for, 12
lecture: with 10–2, 135; Bailey on, 132; at the front of the room, 6, 132; by William James (1892), 119; in Soviet simulation class, 45–46
Lee, Harper, 92
listening: attitude of, 113; barriers to, 126; build respect for, 121; create trust by, 80; paraphrase to encourage, 119; priority as, 133; reading aloud for, 69–70; seeing, experiencing as, 124; students to, 2, 10, 80, 100, 108, 113, 121, 126, 127; Zen of, 127
live action role play (LARP), 71
Lord of the Flies (Golding), 12

The Main Idea (David-Lange), 134
Marshall, Kim, 134
Marshall Memo, 134
Marx, Karl, 35–39, 41; *Communist Manifesto*, 39; description of socialism and capitalism by, 38; dialectical materialism from, 37; on good intellectuals, 36; history as progress by, 27; portrayed as, 46–47, 48; on religion as opiate, 38–39; on structure of capitalist society, 38–39
Mason, Gordon: classroom of, 110; on digital information, 116; on grounded in reality, 119–20; man plowing field of, 106–107; math of, 118; memories of, 119; on Mr. J and phone use, 105, 106–107, 119; for quality of

engagement, 121; teaching as calling, 103; on teaching to change world, 121; turtles all the way down of, 117
master of ceremonies, 5, 10
master teacher, 60, 96, 137
McTighe, Jay, 26
meaning: discover in *Animal Farm*, 10; instilling in students for, 56–57; of life, 20; philosophy having, 99–101; primary sources for, 44; on seeking, 49; students hunger for, 74; students struggle with finding, 89–90, 116
media: on Fox News, 88, 90, 119; RT (Russian TV), 49; soundbites, 88, 89, 90, 109; on students' knowledge of shows, 116; using phones while watching TV, YouTube, 93
"Meet the Communists" panel, 46–47
Meitu (app), 68
mental health days, 134
metaphor: piano teacher as, 12; in poetry, 89; raisin bread as, 117; symphony single note as, 117–18; train station as classroom, 27, 28; turtles all the way down as, 117; whirlpool as, 19
methodological belief, 124–28
methodological doubt, 124–25
Modern History (Becker), 3, 23
Morozov, Pavlov, 16–17
The Mouse and His Child, 69
multitask phone use, 109
Mussolini, Benito, 36
mutual respect, 67, 72

newsletter, 54, 73, 79
non-screen happiness (Twenge), 2

Oldenberg, Martin: embracing controversy of, 77–78; letter to parents, 78–79; on not doing it alone, 78; schools as fiefdoms of, 78; on student expectations, 79; on teaching process, 80; on U.S.–Soviet threat of nuclear war, 80–84
One Day in the Life of Ivan Denisovich (Solzhenitsyn), 92
Orwell, George, 10–12, 79, 109–110

Palmer, Parker, 60
parents: about concern about graphic images, 81; on dinner conversations, 13, 104; filial piety in, 16; on having to call the office, 69; homework help by, 90; letters to, 67, 73, 78–79; on parents' night, 23, 78; portfolio conferences for, 54; "teach" to, 73; teachers as, 3; teachers closer to students than, 7, 130; texting in home by, 110; trust from, 39
personal care, 132
Persons, George: about edge of curriculum, 101–102; on emotional intelligence, 98–99; empathy centerpiece of, 97–98; grading systems of, 52–55, 56; personal philosophy of, 99–100; reputation of, 52; on teaching well, 56–57; on Yondr, 99
petite bourgeoisie, 38
philosophy: Chinese, 15; coming alive as Marx, 35; Confucian, 16, 62; on educational, 37, 65, 90; machine as, 105; on personal, 99–101; significant choice for, 67; Taoist, 18
phones: as addictive, 93, 107, 137; in baskets, cubbies, 39–40, 52, 63, 67, 76, 89, 99, 109; as distractions, 4, 34, 75–76, 88, 89, 93, 126; as elephant in the room, 93; as isolating, 121; for making friends, 107; multitasking with, 109; not in classroom, 3, 7, 22, 37, 69, 71, 72, 88, 108; plowing a field of, 106–107; pockets for, 76, 109; sabbaticals from, 93; shallow processing of, 22, 105, 107, 115; students missing, 9; Turkle on, 1, 7,

8n1, 111; Twenge on, 1–2, 7, 8n3; use in class and home, 63, 72, 108, 127; Yondr for, 88–89, 93,
politically correct mind-set, 116
portfolio, children's work, 54, 62
potential: classroom community, loss of, 71; to diminish students, 13, 60, 109; on false-profile dangers, 68; freeze-dry lessons limit, 100; seek in students, 14, 60, 62–63; teaching to, 100, 115; yellow hat as, 128
The Process of Education: A Searching Discussion of School Education Opening New Paths to Learning and Teaching (Bruner), 62
proletariat, 38–39, 144
propaganda, 42, 72
proverb, Chinese, 56
Pullman, Philip, 69, 74n4
punning, 10, 33
Putin, Vladimir, 49

Ralston, Paula, 66–67, 70–74
Reclaiming Conversation: The Power of Talk in a Digital Age (Turkle), 1
relationships: on administration-teacher, 73–74; on grades as interrupting, 52; to phone as addictive, 93, 107; of teacher-student, 11, 12, 21, 29, 63, 80, 96, 128, 134; of teacher-teacher, 60
religion, 126; as opiate, 38
Rowe, Mary Budd, 132–33
Rowe, Terry: on becoming a teacher, 33–34; growing up of, 34–35; on teaching Marxist socialism, 36–39; on teaching the Soviet Union, 41–48
RT (Russian TV for America), 49
Ruiz, Don Miguel, 134

Sagan, Carl, 114–17, 121n1
Saphier, John, 55

schools: American system of, 65–66; on *Cosmos* perspective, 114; cyberbullying, 108; distractions in, 120; as fiefdoms, 78; Hawkins aim of, 67; improving of, 74, 134; on portfolios for grading, 54; smartphone impact on, 93; as sorting institutions, 16; on Soviet education, 55–56
screen time impact, 1
Shafir, Rebecca, 127
Sharma, Meera: *The Children's Story* of, 14; about classroom management, 4; classroom train station of, 27, 28; on desks in horseshoe, 7–8, 133; for "footprints," 29; internship of, 30; lack of student curiosity, 10; learning of, 12; on Lillian Bailey, 131–32; room setup of, 4; on Turkle and Twenge, 1–2; and you can't do it alone, 135
Singleton, Thomas: methodological believing of, 126; on phone use at home, 127; for six-hat thinking, 129; about students' stubborn point of view, 123, 124
Siri, 105–106
Six Thinking Hats (de Bono), 128–30
Skillful Teacher: Building Your Teaching Skills (Saphier), 55
SMART boards, 4, 67, 76; for conversation, 22; internet on, 39; teaching with, 37, 41, 61
smartphones: in baskets, 52, 99, 109; in cubbies, 39, 67, 109; distraction of, 4, 99; as elephant in the room, 93; on iGen use, 1–2; impact of, 93, 99; less empathy with, 97; overuse of, 108; in pockets, 75–76, 109; for poetry reading, 89; on teen use, 2
Smith, Frances: on ancient Chinese thought, 16–22; for big rocks, 30–31; on Bisaccio final exam, 28; Buddhism, 19; for Confucius analects, 16–18; Confucian analects

by students, 17–18; on early teaching method, 15–16; for "footprints," (McKibben), 28–29; on parent handout, 23; on Suzuki, 17; Taoist sayings by students, 18–19; on teaching for learning, 16; textbook lacking narrative of, 16; for Three Great Ways, 20–22; Winnie the Pooh as a Taoist, 18

Snapchat, 51, 57, 68, 106; addiction to, 4, 93; isolates students, 110

social interaction, 1–2, 97

social media: bombards students, 91; chaos of, 3; on giving up autonomy, 109; in iGen culture, 1; quickens information acquisition, 90

social security, 38

socialism, 35–39, 41, 46, 49; Marxist, 46, 49; preconditions of, 35–37, 41

Solzhenitsyn, Alexander, 92

Soviets: *Animal Farm* of, 10; arms race with, 77, 80–84; "brief history" of, 41–42; on duties of schoolchildren, 43–44; on education system, 55–56; Embassy, 42; Florida-Cuba dam, 13; on inculcating communism in 1960s, 37, 39, 48–49; on Pavlov Morozov, 16–17; simulated classroom, 44–48; teaching about, 41–49;

Stalin, Joseph, 48–49; portrayed as, 46–47

standardized tests: on drill-and-kill prep, 56; end of the year, 22, 68, 78; grouping by, 66

standards: able to avoid, 10, 62, 68, 78, 79; Common Core, 80; on holding high, 62, 63; pressure to meet, 15, 95; about setting, when planning, 73; stay close to, 76

"staying on the same page" mindset, 101

step aside, 132

stock exchange, 62

students: affirmation of, 60; backward design perspective on, 26–27; before smartphones, 3; as biologists, 28; caring about, 5, 26, 56, 60, 63, 67, 82, 91, 108; conservatory (Zander), 54; as detectives, 41–43; empathy in, 44, 97, 98; engagement of, 74, 121, 123–24; expectations for, 79; fairness to, 4–5; former students as Marxist revolutionaries, 49; as good intellectuals, 36; on grades used to sort, 15–16, 55; as guests, 19, 92–93; as historians, 28; invitations to, 19–22, 55, 73, 97, 110; lack of vocabulary in, 88–89; listen to, 33, 60, 61, 80, 108, 110, 127; making choices by, 66, 67; as Marx's "the vanguard," 36–37; as Marxist petite bourgeoise oppressors, 38; for open environment, 66, 68–69; on phones, 4, 75–76, 88–89, 93, 97, 107–108; prodding students to read, 91–92; raisins as galaxies with, 117; on screen-based apathy of students, 52; see what is (Krishnamurti), 90–91; Soviet simulated classroom for, 44–48; as stakeholders, 22, 55, 57, 133; texting preference by, 7, 51, 88; in tracked classes, 12–13; in train station, 27, 28; as unique, 10

study habits, 55

Suzuki, Shunryu, 17, 22

Swimme, Brian, 115, 117–18, 120

Symons, Jennifer, 66–68, 71–74

tablets, 7, 27, 61, 67, 76, 115, 119

The Tao of Pooh (Hoff), 18

Tao Te Ching (Tzu), 18

teachers: administrators dropping in classrooms, 95–96; asking for help for, 134; as backbone, 130; calling as, 3, 103; considering the long view of, 25–26; creative as, 5, 52; as deciders, 109; as deliverers, 5, 15, 66, 110, 118; evaluating students' through writing, 17, 118;

evaluation of, 79, 95–96, 120; good relationships with students, 11–12, 21, 60, 63, 80, 96, 99, 128, 134; having a good relationship with administrators, 73–74; on learning happen in classroom, 12, 23, 54, 125; letters from, 67, 73, 78–79; as noble profession, 5, 90; on parents' evenings in classroom, 73; path to, 2–3; piano teacher metaphor of, 12; treating students as persons, 7, 10, 11, 93;

teaching: on 10–2, 97, 132, 135; accessing TV and internet, 120; as in big rocks, 30–31; to change the world, 121; children come first in, 67; complexity of, 26, 79, 100, 101; as delivering, 5, 15–16, 66, 85, 110, 118, 120; on desks in horseshoe, 7, 9, 10, 133; as dog-and-pony show, 54, 78, 120; as doing the learning, 12; early years of, 9–10; on flipped classroom, 16; focus on facts not fiction, 119–20; framing big picture for, 25–31; at the front of the room, 6, 15, 42, 133; as fun, 11; about good, 22, 53, 60, 100; good management of, 4; on honest, 100; about I/D/I planning, 73; immersion for, 37, 41; invitations as, 19–22, 55, 66, 73, 97, 100, 110; as joyous, 100; as life, 23; for lifelong learning, 29, 100, 101; on mental health days, 134; methodological belief for, 124–28; as noble calling, 90–91; on parents, 23, 54, 73, 78–79, 90, 105, 134; passion for, 34, 66, 103, 115; path to, 2; personal emphasis in, 1, 11, 20, 22, 72; philosophy of, 99–101; phone issues for, 2, 9, 34, 75, 88–89, 93, 99, 105, 106–109, 115; preparation for, 5, 30, 37, 101; process of, 80, 90, 91, 97, 119; quality of, 29; on role plays, 91; on routine classroom delivery, 2, 5, 78, 120; as satisfying, 100; on seeing students anew every day, 63; as show, 4, 61; six thinking hats for, 128–30; on Soviet, 55–56; testing as wrong mind-set, 56; triads for, 90, 97; understanding for, 10–11, 19ff, 26–27, 56–57, 100–101, 117–18; on Zen listening, 127

textbooks: in the closet, 23; comparative use of, 121; curriculum as, 5, 27, 76; obsolete information in, 119; opposition to, 5, 23;

texting: avoids personal interaction, 72; avoids reflection, 90; incessant, 108; in the home, 110–11; isolates people, 110; student use during class, 4; students' preference for, 7, 51, 88

Thomas, Dylan, 89

threat of grades, 53

"Three Good Things" (UC Berkeley), 98

"Three Great Ways," 20–22; Brother Christopher, Sister Carolyn, and Teacher Francis in, 20; four questions of, 20

Through the Looking Glass (Carroll), 127

Tiddely Pom Principle, 18

The Tipping Point (Gladwell), 51

To Kill a Mockingbird (Lee), 92, 97

tracking: in AP, 13; classes by, 12–14, 23, 60; top section on, 53

triads, 97

Trotsky, Leon, portrayed as, 46–47

trust, 61, 63, 73, 80

Turkle, Sherry, 1, 7, 111

Turning to One Another: Simple Conversations to Restore Hope to the Future (Wheatley), 110

"turtles all the way down" mind-set, 117

Twenge, Jean M., 1–2, 7

Twitter, 51

Ulyanov, Vladimir Ilyich (Lenin): with cap, 34; *Iskra*, 45; portrayed as, 46–48
Understanding by Design (Wiggins and McTighe), 26
The Universe Story: From the Primordial Flaring Forth to the Ecozoic Era–A Celebration of the Unfolding of the Cosmos (Berry, Swimme), 121n4

wait time, 132–33
Watson, Amy: build respect through listening, 121; on classroom distractions, 120; cyberbullying of, 108; digital-audio invasions of, 106; on freedom behind closed door 120; on listening to students, 113, 119; on metaphors as centerpiece, 118; on Mr. J, 119; about politically correct, 116; tablets, Google Drive, of, 119; teaching as calling, 103
"We teach who we are" (Palmer), 60
"What the Internet is Doing to Our Brains," (Carr), 107

Wheatley, Margaret, 110, 113, 119
Wiggins, Grant, 26
Wilson, Jeremy: administration relationship with, 74–75; classroom as community, 71; on invitations to learn, 73; letter to Lewis Denton, 58–74; on parents, 74; for planning model (I/D/I), 73; portrayal apps of, 68
Winnie the Pooh, 18
Witney Café, 1, 15, 25, 131
"wonderfully curious" (Fried), 108, 111n3
workplace mind-set, 74
Wu Wei, 18

Xentano Café, 40, 41

YouTube, 37, 39–40, 89

Zander, Benjamin, 54
Zen Mind, Beginner's Mind (Suzuki), 17
The Zen of Listening (Shafir), 127

About the Author

Frank Thoms, a lifelong teacher and consultant, smiles when he hears former students tell him, "You taught me how to think, Mr. Thoms." From his earliest days in his classroom, he has probed the minds and hearts of his students. He created countless approaches in his classroom for nearly forty years as a teacher and twelve years as an educational consultant. "Don't do tomorrow what I did today" became his mantra.

He is the author of three books. The first he self-published: *Teaching from the Middle of the Room: Inviting Students to Learn* (2010). The other two were published by Rowman & Littlefield: *Teaching That Matters: Engaging Minds, Improving Schools* (2014) and *Exciting Classrooms: Practical Information to Ensure Student Success* (2015). His writing focuses on teachers making learning happen in the classroom rather than standing before students delivering information. It is a simple distinction with broad implications.

The bulk of his teaching occurred in the twentieth century, but he is conversant on the impact of digital technology on today's students, enough so that his current writing addresses his concerns. And he's an advocate of connecting generations of teachers. Staying connected strengthens the profession. Hence this book, *Listening Is Learning: Conversations between 20th and 21st Century Teachers*.

You can contact Frank at frankthoms3@gmail.com and visit his website at www.frankthoms.com. He would welcome your comments about this book and other thoughts about teaching and learning.

www.ingramcontent.com/pod-product-compliance
Lightning Source LLC
Chambersburg PA
CBHW030139240426
43672CB00005B/195